What People Are Saying About Dr. Courtney Linsenmeyer - O'Brien, Ph.D., MHR, PLC

I have known Dr. O'Brien for more than 25 years, both as a friend and a colleague. I have had the opportunity to watch her personal and career growth over those years, now culminating in this informative and useful book on the challenging subject of the narcissist.

I met her first as an excellent personal trainer, something she achieved after many physical challenges that would have defeated others. She guided me to a major transformation of my body and taught me much about how to maintain my physical self, something that has become even more important with the passing years. During that time, she was a keen observer of human behavior, increasingly becoming interested in how she could mentally and emotionally impact lives as well as the physical impact.

This led to her pursuit of a doctorate (with an emphasis on the studies leading to this book) and the opening of her clinical practice. She pursued these goals with the same passion as her initial personal training pursuit.

This book is in particular about the covert narcissist. This is something I am familiar with as a board-certified psychiatrist, but mostly in assessment rather than ongoing treatment due to the fact that such individuals rarely stay in treatment. The problem is always someone else's and confronting this distortion leads to departure from treatment.

The book is thus not about how to treat a narcissist, but how to recognize one. It is written primarily in layman's words rather than clinical words, making it easier to use as a guide. For those individuals who find themselves in a significant relationship with one, it is about a journey toward recognition of how that narcissist has affected them, damaged and distorted their sense of self, made them believe that all the relationship problems are of their making. Often they become too demoralized to see the full picture or to believe that they can remove themselves from the situation and rebuild their own healthier lives. Because the narcissist will not own any responsibility or agree to make changes, most often the only healthy way to salvage one's life is to find the courage to end the relationship and begin a new path, but that requires understanding, hope, and trust in oneself to undertake. Sadly, some never trust themselves enough to do so. But for those who are looking to be enlightened, and who want to find their way to a life that they control, not the narcissist, this book is a guide that can change their lives.

Dr. Dwight Holden, MD.
AMERICAN BOARD OF PSYCHIATRY
AND NEUROLOGY (Psychiatry specific)

Dr. Courtney O'Brien does a masterful job providing insight into the complex nature of Covert Narcissism and the toxic and often destructive power it has on others. The trauma inflicted by the Covert Narcissist can leave victims broken, feeling intense shame and guilt, even questioning one's own sanity. Through her vast knowledge and experience, Dr. O'Brien provides a beacon of hope to victims, family members, and friends of the those caught up in the destructive tornado of the Narcissist. This book is a must read for those supporting victims and offers hope and healing that it can get better.

Chan M Hellman, PhD
Professor – Anne & Henry Zarrow School of Social Work
Director – Hope Research Center
University of Oklahoma
http://www.ou.edu/tulsa/hope

As a layman, I never realized the enormity of problems that exist as a result of being in the company of a Covert narcissist, much less being subject to the consequences of their behavior. Before I read the book, I never gave much thought to narcissism let alone, what a narcissist is capable of doing to another person.

It opened my eyes to the dangers that arise as a result of being in the presence of a Covert narcissist. After reading the book, what I did not know now makes sense. What may seem to be a normal behavior on the surface is not always the truth.

Thank you, Dr. O'Brien.

James W. Barlow, ESQ

WORKING TOWARDS A BRIGHTER REALITY

An Honest Approach to Understanding the Narcissist

Dr. Courtney Linsenmeyer - O'Brien, Ph.D, MHR, PLC

www.TotalPublishingAndMedia.com

WORKING TOWARDS A BRIGHTER REALITY
An Honest Approach to Understanding the Narcissist

Is an original publication of TOTAL PUBLISHING AND MEDIA.
This work has never before appeared in book form.

Copyright © 2023 by:
Dr. Courtney Linsenmeyer-Obrien, PH.D.MHR, PLC
ISBN: 978-1-63302-256-0

All rights reserved. No part of this publication may be reproduced, distributed, or transmitted in any form or by any means, including photocopying, recording, or other electronic or mechanical methods, or any information storage and retrieval systems, without the prior written permission of the publisher, except in the case of brief quotations embodied in critical reviews and certain other noncommercial uses permitted by copyright law.

Request for permission to make copies of any part of this
work should be mailed to

TOTAL PUBLISHING AND MEDIA
5411 South 125th East Ave.
Suite 302
Tulsa, Ok. 74146
www.totalpublihingandmedia.com

Printed in the United States of America

FIRST EDITION

DISCLAIMER

This book is for informational purposes only. It is not intended to be used in place of one-on-one professional advice, therapeutic treatments for mental health disorders, diagnostic assessments, medical treatment, or professional oversight in any way. It should not be used in lieu of professional guidance or as a medium to self-diagnoses. Please consult with a qualified physician or healthcare provider before changing any health care regimen. All names have been changed to protect the privacy of the individuals in this book.

DEDICATIONS

"I would like to dedicate this book to my clients who have suffered through painful relationships with narcissists and who had the courage to seek help. It is through your bravery and stories this book was birthed. And to Jamie Bohannon who has been as much a part of this book as I have. You are the best support staff I have had in my fifteen years of practice. For this and so much more I am forever grateful."

TABLE OF CONTENTS

Chapter 1: A BRIEF LOOK INTO NARCISSISM 1
   The Narcissist Bully..13
   Personal Relationships 16
   Fear Bombing vs Love Bombing..............................18
   Scripting Relationships/Creating Their Own Reality 20
   A Pathological Narcissist 20
   Online Sexual Behaviors and The Narcissist............22
   Using Sex to Control...23
   Insanity and Gaslighting/A Mindfuck........................25

Chapter 2: DROWNING IN YOUR OWN BLOOD! 31
   Episodic Erruptions...32
   Covert vs Overt Narcissists.......................................33
   I Hate You Don't Leave Me!.....................................36
   You Say That You Love Me But Do Not Show It....37
   Things A Narcissist Fears Most 37
   A Mass of Self-Doubt 47
   The Rage and Massacre 45
   Triangulation...49
   Guilt and Shame..51

Chapter 3: WHY COLLECT PEOPLE? 53
   Love Bombing 54
   Domestic Financial Abuse 57
   Narcisssts and Co-Dependency 62
   Can Narcissists Change? 64
   The Drug Dealer in Disguise 66
   Hoarding People 79

Chapter 4: INTIMACY AND SEXUALITY 83
   Justifying Infidelity 88
   Finding Religion 91
   Forgiveness 92
   Forgive Yourself 94
   The Narcissist and Parental Control 95
   Projecting: A Dangerous Relationship 98

Chapter 5: EMOTIONAL INCEST 101
   Children Becoming a Surrogate Spouse
      to the Narcissist Parent 109

Chapter 6: TRAUMA BONDING 111
   Emotionally Abandoning the Marriage 113
   Punishing the Spouse 114
   Parent/Child Alienation 115

Chapter 7: WHEN YOU REALIZE,
      YOU ARE MARRIED TO A NARICSSIST 123
   Divorcing A Narcissist 126
   Healthy Narcissism 129
   A Narcissist's Fear of the Therapy Room 131
   Are You More Afraid of Leaving or Staying
      in an Unhealthy Relationship? 139

Why Would Anyone Stay in an Unhealthy
    Relationship if They Knew it was Unhealthy? 141
Emotional Abuse and the Impact of Staying 143
Pulling the Trigger 145

Chapter 8: HOW TO HEAL 147
    Facing Your Fear of Change: Be Honest With Yourself 149
    Let Them Have Their Glory 163
    Finding Love After Healing 166
    Trust Your Instincts 168
    Learn Faith 169

Conclusion 171

ACKNOWLEDGEMENTS

I would like to thank those who have given me the encouragement to complete this book. It has been a long journey due to the many excuses we use to put off completing a long-term goal. I will begin by thanking my undergraduate professors for being the people who showed me how to navigate the beginning of my academic career. You helped me believe in myself on a journey that felt endless and doubtful at times. At one time or another, all of you came to know an education felt like a fairytale to me. Dr. Holmes, thank you for your encouragement and support during the endless compositions written near the end of my master's graduate research. Your investment in me and shared classic journals gave me a deeper understanding of psychology, and human relations. Lastly, thank you for gifting me your priceless collection of Abraham Maslow's writings. I am forever grateful.

Thank you to Dr. Amedeo Giorgi for heading my Dissertation Board. I will always be grateful to you for providing me with the opportunity to conduct research overseas with you. Hearing you speak in countries outside of the United States was an honor and experience I will never forget. I would also like to thank Dr. Stanley Krippner, PhD., and Dr. Ruth Richards, MD, PhD. Dr. Richards, you were an inspiration to me and a woman whom I could only hope to follow. Your work as a psychiatrist, Fellow of the American Psychological Association, author, and feminist researcher was beyond influential. You were so far ahead of your time I cannot imagine your journey to success. Your passion and persistence to make waves and success happen for women in academia and beyond was amazing to watch. Your work and research live on through the walls of Harvard, Berkley, and all of us who were touched by your life. You are always with me in spirit. Dr. Krippner, you made my research and writing fun, yet challenging. Your demands to write well were absolute and carried forward with an iron fist. Thank you for this. It has given me a higher standard by which to measure my skills and achieve success.

To all of you who sat on my dissertation board, thank you for pulling no punches to assure I earned the credentials which now follow my name. I would also like to thank those who vicariously traveled on this journey with me through inquisitive conversations and your genuine interest. You gave me an outlet to hear myself think and feedback which helped me navigate my career choices. I would also like to thank Jamie Bohannon who has been my office administrator for many years. You have been instrumental in helping me grow my practice and juggle the many balls I throw at you every day. Being on the frontline of the day-to-day tasks and interactions is a job I cannot imagine or want to step into. You make what seems to be impossible, possible.

Lastly, I am grateful to my mother and family who never gave up on me through tough times of sickness and brain surgery. I cannot imagine the stressful days and nights which ensued as a result of caring for an epileptic child. This book would not be possible without my mother. I am forever beholden to you for your emotional support as a child now an adult.

PREFACE

I began writing this book early in my career. It has been slow to unfold due to the common excuses we all make at one time or another to put a task or goal on hold. However, the timing was a blessing, as I was able to experience life in a way that would make this book a reality and engrain myself in my career which eventually brought truth to the words within the book. I have learned that words are healing and there is life after being trapped in a relationship which seems impossible to escape. This lesson is both personal and professional. It would not be possible to grow and thrive in my mental health practice without learning of the personal stories and experiences embedded in narcissistic relationships.

I believe it is important to mention that my career in mental health was given life when I worked as a personal trainer. I jokingly say my career began at this point in my life, because after ten years in the training business, I realized (although people hired me to help them change their overall lifestyle by exercising and eating healthier), they continued to see me for the trusted relationship birthed through the hours of pumping iron on a gym floor. Their physical health goals soon fell second to their personal desire or need to talk about their problems. Struggles with kids, spouse, career, self-esteem, and anything they felt comfortable disclosing – for which they could not discuss with another person were part of the session. I was the landscape for people to share secrets, shame, lies, insecurities, abuse, and the elements woven into a co-dependent relationship. The trenches of trauma and relationship frustrations were embedded in the physical exertion of a leg extension or overhead shoulder press. The adrenaline from exercise coupled with a person in need of empathy, understanding, and a desire to be heard worked symbiotically to provide a safe place where confidentiality and unconditional trust would propel self-disclosure. It was a perfect example of how the mind needs the body and the body needs the mind to achieve optimal health; especially when emotional pain feels all consuming.

Before I move on, it is important to say I embraced my job as a trainer and cared deeply for my clients. However, while the discovery of these relationships was important to understand and necessary to learn to navigate, I did not always enjoy every client. You might say some people were obnoxious, self-important, and disillusioned by their self-importance. It was interesting to learn how many life stories had been embellished and even untrue. These people wanted to hire an ear who would listen to them talk about their claim to fame or add to their collection of people who made them appear successful. Gaining the approval and acceptance from those who also had their own person trainer was common. A client might speak of their days as a college athlete, being the best 6th grade soccer player in the nation, buying one-of-a kind possessions, being known for their greatness, or be braggadocios about the people in their lives for the purpose of elevating themselves. I quickly learned patience.

If you are in a relationship with a narcissist, you already know managing self-love requires knowing how to mirror and quietly tolerate their ego to avoid conflict. Adapting to the moment became a skill and how I learned to create necessary boundaries which would ultimately provide a safe zone. Knowing how to navigate emotions was important. Furthermore, being present in the moment helped provide healthy communication, establish boundaries, and avoid conflict. If we are talking about someone your gut does not trust, difficult to tolerate, highly emotional, manipulative, or worse, an emotional predator, survival is about self-preservation during the communication process.

This book would not be complete, and I would be leaving a huge gap in its purpose if I did not mention that I have a very intimate understanding of what it is like to live with a narcissist and feel the bondage of emotional control and manipulation. I have survived and am now thriving. Although I have both a professional and very personal understanding of narcissistic abuse, the stories within this book explain it best. It is my hope to help you identify narcissistic behavior and validate your suspicions regarding abuse, entrapment, emotional control, and toxicity within a relationship. I believe you will be closer to gaining the power it takes to propel freedom and rebuild your life. Knowledge, encouragement, and self-confidence will help you heal as you create a stronger, smarter, and less vulnerable person within.

AUTHOR'S NOTE

The word narcissism is used often in today's environment and has even become a trendy word to describe someone who is arrogant or self-righteous. Although this may apply, it is not that simple. Please understand narcissism goes much deeper than this, as it victimizes people who struggle to regain their lives after they have been affected by a narcissistic abuser.

Although this book is about narcissism, it's focus is on the most dangerous type of narcissist which is the covert narcissist. A covert narcissist is someone who uses forms of emotional and psychological manipulation to control and manipulate you. The most abusive aspect about these narcissists is they use control and abuse you in ways which go unseen. This means they appear to be looking out for your best interest when they are tearing you apart from the inside. They trick you into believing things which are not true, blame you for their mistakes, lack empathy, and can even make you feel as if you are losing your mind. Their victims suffer anxiety, depression, isolation, self-abuse, and even commit suicide. Although the abuse is horrid, victims report watching a narcissist convince people they are good people, and align themselves with the narcissist, is maddening and lonely. You can and will find freedom if you take it.

"Narcissists are soul rapists. They brutally violate our right to be happy in our own skin. Not because we have done something wrong, but just because we are alive."
– Milva

Accept what is, let go of what was, and gain the power to propel your own future.
– Dr. Linsenmeyer-O'Brien, PhD.

WHY READ THIS BOOK?

Working Towards a Brighter Reality: An Honest Approach to Understanding the Narcissist will provide an understanding of narcissism and allow you to see what it looks like in a relationship. It puts words and meaning to the reality of narcissistic abuse and healing. The content within and true stories of victims bring validation to the reality of narcissistic abuse. This book uncovers the reasons why narcissists control at the expense of others and exposes the insecurities masked by a narcissist's display of self-confidence. More importantly, it will provide hope when there seems no way out and encourage you to embrace faith in your own way to change your life.

INTRODUCTION

Dr. O'Brien was challenged by many obstacles in her youth and adult life by health conditions beyond her control. At the age of six, she was diagnosed with a rare disease which nearly took her life. Encephalitis is a disease caused by severe fever resulting in inflammation of the brain and eventual death if not treated. Brain damage caused uncontrollable seizures for which medication failed to control. Comas were not uncommon when ongoing seizures would cluster. Embarrassment, shame, and fear of failure controlled her life due to the unpredictability of losing consciousness during a conversation or worse, experiencing a sudden convulsive seizure. The educational environment was overwhelming and cognitive processing was impossible due to the brain damage caused by encephalitis and comas.

Academics were torture and failing grades ensued as a result. Reading clinics, tutors, and independent meetings with teachers were of no help and only made her feel stupid and inadequate. She found a purpose in sports and believes athletics was the only reason she graduated from high school. She would enter college at Oklahoma State University where her father played basketball for Henry IBA during the National Championships. It was only because of this she went to college. She quit school her sophomore year to marry a man her mother decided was, "The One" to marry. Her mother was fearful she would not be capable of caring for herself due to neurological issues caused by encephalitis. Unfortunately, seizures continued to prevent her from furthering her education or securing a job. However, years into the marriage, medical opportunities presented a chance to be free from the control of seizures. After months of living on an epilepsy ward at the Mayo Clinic in Minneapolis, it was determined she was a candidate for brain surgery.

It would be one of the biggest decisions she would make due to the chance of death, memory loss, paralysis, or further unknown brain damage. After a long thought process and weighing the costs and benefits, she had a right temporal lobectomy. Explained another way, she no longer has a right temporal lobe. Her left temporal lobe functions as both the right and left lobe. After a long journey back to health, Dr. O'Brien no longer has seizures. It would be two years into her neurological rehabilitation she learned to drive in her twenties. Without an education or a history of work, she got a job throwing newspapers at 5:00am for the Tulsa World newspaper and The Tulsa Tribune. It was good driving practice, as there were no cars on the road. She also taught aerobics during the day at a Jewish Community Center and local hospital. This led her into a world of personal training for the next 10 years.

Because she came from a family of athletes and enjoyed physical activity, she became competitive in body building. Dr. O'Brien notes, "This was the best time in my life because I was finally free from the prison of being an epileptic." "I finally had the opportunity to get an education, know the freedom felt when driving a car, and become financially independent." She went on to say, "My biggest fear was being controlled by someone and not having the resources to leave, should I be in danger." That said, Dr. O'Brien used her time as a trainer to facilitate a return to college and finish her undergraduate degree, while continuing her master's and Doctorate degree. Dr. O'Brien said, "This was the most prudent decision I have ever made." "My education gave me the self-confidence I needed to carry on despite past feelings of intellectual inadequacy caused by my epilepsy." "More importantly, it gave me the power to make my own decisions while helping those who struggle with feeling trapped, unloved, controlled, and victimized by others." A degree does not make you smart or suggest you are better than others. It breeds confidence, grows self-esteem, and provides a foundation no one can take from you. Most importantly, it reminds you there is always someone smarter than you.

CHAPTER 1

A BRIEF LOOK INTO NARCISSISM

Being the object of a Narcissist's self-love is not something you may recognize or even believe, until you are overwhelmed with anxiety. Perhaps your feelings of distress are mistakenly identified as something outside of the narcissist relationship. This can be confusing and cause you to overlook the toxic realities of living with the person whom you have come to trust, admire, and love. The chances of your anxiety being symptomatic of anything other than the pain caused by the narcissist is slim to none. It is like trying to convince yourself the sun orbits the earth. It is important to mention early on that admiration for the narcissist can be mistaken for the fascination of the narcissist's charisma and accomplished persona. It is easy to let their fake display of self-confidence and compelling charm elicit idolatry. This trap is easy to fall into because it is human nature to crave emotional connection and acceptance from others. In the beginning, their presence feels good, safe, and maybe even exhilarating. People will say such things as, "He started verbally abusing me after we got married," "He tries to make me jealous in pubic then tells me I am insecure," "His personality changed after we moved in together." These are warning signs which indicate the narcissist is trying to gain power in the relationship. The narcissist will likely use you to gain attention, accumulate relationships, and feel important. For the sake of the stories in this book, I would like to note that according to (Stinson et al, 2008, pg. 1), narcissism effects 7.7% of males and 4.8% of females in the general population. It is not my intention to discriminate against men.

    A narcissist's life journey for endless affirmation can be exhausting for those who serve as their emotional supplier and can become treacherous if the narcissist's ideas, or intentions are questioned. They avoid people who disagree or are suspicious of their motives. Instead, the narcissist will capitalize on opportunities which will convince others of their perceived greatness. This could sound like someone who is just annoying and could be easily ignored, but the narcissist is relentless at convincing others they are right. They seek out, (and allure) those who are unassuming, easily influenced, and people who desire to learn from them. They can quickly zone in on this person and capitalize on the chance to gain their admiration. Their preferred emotional playing field is with those who are not likely to question their motives. These individuals tend to be those who may need to learn from the narcissist, (such as an employee or child) who automatically trusts the narcissist due the natural order of power within the context of the relationship. Furthermore, the narcissist survives and thrives on the passive personality and those who may be seeking acceptance or love after a lost relationship. They love opportunities which fill the space of emptiness in people who are struggling with emotional transition. This includes the person who has lost a loved one, made poor investment choices, exiting a relationship, or at a confusing impasse in life. We have all had challenges which have made us feel temporarily stuck, hopeless, weak, or like a failure. This makes *everyone* a target to the narcissist because the unique aspect about a narcissist's choice of victim is ultimately rooted in your overall ability to be manipulated. Vulnerability and circumstances which are situationally opportunistic give the narcissistic the space and opportunity to manipulate and control. This is seen in the Covid-19 stories below and the stories that follow.

Not everyone who suffers loss or experiences emotional trauma can be manipulated by a narcissist. In fact, the narcissists will stay away from people who do not immediately think they are great or question their intent.

THE COVID-19 PANDEMIC OF 2020

Life as we know it will never be the same after living through the 2019 pandemic in the United States. When the prison doors of Covid-19 locked behind all of us, emotional turmoil hovered over every life to varying degrees. For those of us in the mental health business, we still see its effects as we turn people away because we do not have time to help everyone in need. The Pandemic blew the lid off struggling relationships. Relationship issues which had not yet risen or life problems locked away, suddenly surfaced to an undeniable reality. This created an immediate and desperate rise in people seeking help with their lives and relationships. This is because the Pandemic pulled the covers off relational problems hidden, ignored, denied, or that quietly existed in a vacuum. It also made current issues more noticeable, harder to ignore, and more likely to implode due to the constant presence of spoken or unspoken emotional conflict. An inability to escape the issues only made it worse. People where stuck with themselves and each other, desperately seeking new ways to adapt. More specifically, liars were caught red-handed in their lies, addicts were unable to successfully navigate their addictions, cheaters were exploited by their lover's insecurities or compulsions, and spouses who were contemplating divorce finally pulled the trigger. One of the most devastating outcomes has been the effect the pandemic had on victims of emotional and physical abuse. Victims were suddenly closer to their abusers without the ability to emotionally or physically escape. Living in the same home with an abuser of any kind is tragic. Being trapped with a narcissist who is emotionally abusive is torture. Emotionally abused victims became the sole source of the narcissist's ego. What narcissist supply could not be sourced out through social media was dumped onto the closest person in the home who was the most vulnerable and easiest to control. This person became the primary feed box to nurse the neurosis of the narcissist's personality – without the ability to establish a "safe space." People suffered greatly as the gates of Covid-19 closed in on their personal freedoms. However, once everyone settled into their homes and adapted to seclusion, people flocked to mental health professionals as soon as the world quickly shifted to virtual communication. The Pandemic has changed the platform of communication forever and allowed people to get help who would not or could not get help Pre-Pandemic. Medical practices, medicine, and the mental health field will never be the same and are more accessible now than ever. Because of Covid-19, victims of narcissistic abuse can get the professional help they need within a safe space and minimize the risks associated with acting outside of their abuser's control.

MADDIE AND HER DAD – JERRY

Jerry is a father of three and husband of 30 years to his high school sweetheart. Kale is their oldest child and attends college at an Ivy league school on the East Coast. He loves the college, girls, and his fraternity. Juna is the middle child and plays in the Chicago Symphony. She has no plans to return home. Maddie is the youngest child and hopes to become a chemical engineer. She was approaching graduation from a private high school not far from their home in Connecticut. She played varsity basketball, volleyball, and maintained a 4.0 academic average. Maddie learned commitment, fortitude, and faith in herself would propel her success after completing high school. However, she often felt anxious when around her father, complained he was too strict, and focused too much on how she looked. He often made comments which made her second guess her decisions and feel ashamed of herself. Examples are below:

- "Are you really going to eat that?"
- "I never really cared for sugar because it makes us fat."
- "You should think more about what you wear." "Some clothes make you look so unattractive."
- "Have you changed something about yourself?" "You look different."

She would spend hours in her room crying and looking in the mirror feeling shameful about her body and inability to make her dad proud. She looked forward to the day she could get away from her father's emotional abuse. This became a reality when she was accepted to UC Berkeley on an academic scholarship. The news came one week before Covid-19 shut the world down and the country went into isolation. Panic attacks, depression, suicide, and a fear of death, (in one way or another), dominated the mental wellness of most people. In this case, Maddie was no exception. Like all of those who lived with abuse during this time, Maddie was confined to her father's abuse, and his control became cripplingly. Her anxiety escalated and locking herself in her closet became routine. If she was not in her closet, she locked herself in her bedroom. She said, "I felt, worthless, ugly, and as if I did not deserve my academic scholarship to Berkeley." Maddie's father tried to sabotage her pursuits to keep her within his control and at home with him. He once said, "I was offered a scholarship to an Ivy league school but did not take it because I felt an obligation to stay home and take care of my parents." Jerry was using guilt to make his daughter question her decision to go to Berkeley. Narcissists can and will take advantage of any opportunity to get their needs met. For many, the Covid-19 restrictions enabled this. Maddie's father also made comments like: "You should take a minute or two to commit, as you may regret it later." Or: "Although this is a wonderful opportunity, it will be challenging, and you may lose your close friendships." Her father's advice was said to make her second guess her decision to accept the scholarship and impose fear and doubt as to her value while questioning her academic pursuits. In some instances, this was a narcissist's dream. Many narcissists had a host of people (or a person) held captive who could become a source of their ego supply while using emotional vulnerability to feel in control. As I previously mentioned, I am happy to say Covid-19 caused a massive shift in the field of mental health by opening the floodgates of communication for those trapped in their homes feeling hopeless and helpless. Maddie eventually took advantage of virtual media and telemedicine to get the therapy and help she needed. She did this without her father knowing as she spent time locked in her bedroom on a virtual call. She is now at school in California and away from her father's control. She is learning to recognize narcissistic traits to avoid befriending someone like her father. Equally important, she is attending trauma seminars and going to support groups for those who suffer from emotional abuse.

I think about Maddie from time to time, as she was a very broken young girl who was the source of her father's ego supply, insecurities, and his emotional abuse for which she could not see or speak about until she could weed through the webs of emotional abuse which kept her trapped in his clutches. She is free and no longer the subject of her father's domination.

Nathan and Piper

Nathan and Piper met at a wedding in Arizona. They both knew the groom and flew from different states to attend. The groom was a fraternity brother of Nathan's and a high school friend of Piper's. Nathan saw Piper from across the room while at the reception. She did not appear to be with anyone and was not wearing a wedding ring. She was beautiful. Nathan approached her and began to talk about how well he knew the groom and the groom's family. He also shared his experiences as a pilot and described the wonderful and exotic places he had visited while flying. He said "He loved the lifestyle piloting allowed and was going to buy his own plane soon." Piper was impressed and shared that she just passed the Bar exam and was preparing to practice family law. It was not soon before Nathan and Piper were visiting one another from their separate homes in different states. They were approaching the one-year mark of long-distance dating and Nathan felt it was time to discuss being together full time. This meant one person would need to move locations. Piper was trying to determine if it made more sense for her to move or if Nathan should move. As a pilot, Nathan could live most anywhere, and her law practice had not yet been established. However, Piper's family was near as were her friends. Nathan did not have family in one central location, and he did not have much of a relationship with them. This did not seem to matter, as Nathan convinced Piper to move by assuring her they would visit her family often and emphasized that her law practice would thrive in his part of the world. She trusted Nathan and moved to be with him, and then Covid-19 happened. The time spent in isolation with Nathan was horrible and eye-opening. Piper quickly learned Nathan was not a pilot and had not been out of the country. He was in debt, spent his money on car payments he could not afford and on things which made others believe he was successful. Gucci shoes, Prada suits, Giorgio Armani shirts, and a Rolex watch – all of which were knockoffs, as he could only afford fakes. Everything was a lie, and she was trapped. The pandemic spawned a minefield of psychological issues which affected Piper's ability to be emotionally safe and financially independent. She did not have the means to support herself and realized she had been manipulated. Nathan was an imposter whom she did not know. One year later, she is still with Nathan who does not approve of her desire to seek counseling. I have faith she will find her way to freedom and hope to hear from her someday.

Jennifer and Michelle

Michelle met Jennifer at a social event organized to support women and minorities. They made a connection and determined meeting one another was meant to be. Both women identified as lesbian from an early age, agreed on most social issues, and were raised in the Christian church. Jennifer was a court reporter and Michelle traveled the United States speaking on behalf of women who had been abused or who were in an abusive relationship. Both women were independent, intelligent, and more than capable of financially supporting themselves. Michelle was outgoing and felt her best when she was on stage speaking. Jennifer was reserved, optimistic, and spent a great deal of time with her family. Both women felt as if they completed each other – that was until Jennifer discovered text messages between Michelle and a male lover during the COVID-19 Pandemic. Jennifer was in shock. She could not believe this had happened. Did Michelle have an epiphany which opened her eyes to new a sexual identity? If so, why did she not discuss her feelings with Jennifer? Michelle was a sex addict. She was able to hide this from Jennifer because she traveled. Cheating made Michelle feel powerful and not responsible for Jennifer's feelings. It was fun, risky, euphoric, and gender or sexual identity was not a factor in her pursuits. Wendy Behary states, in her book, "Disarming the Narcissist, Surviving & Thriving with the Self-Absorbed," "Narcissists search for detached self-stimulation when not engaged in other distractions or holding court can lead them to seek out quick highs that eventually may become enduring addictions, including sex addictions." Jennifer was devastated and felt like a fool. She was embarrassed and disappointed in herself. She left Michelle once the chaos from the pandemic subsided. Before she left she had endured verbal abuse and Michelle blamed her for her circumstance. Michelle told Jennifer, "If you were a better lover and partner, I would have been faithful." Jennifer said, "Had it not been for my strength and persistence to change my situation through virtual therapy, I believe I could be trapped in an abusive relationship." One month later, Jennifer heard Michelle moved into the home of a male who she met online during covid.

Emry and her Boss

Emry was a young woman raised by her grandmother because her parents where unstable and often absent from her life. They lived in a poor area of Kansas and had a difficult time paying for groceries and the monthly bills. They often had to choose between the two. Emry struggled with anxiety, depression, and had fears of the future that became irrational at times. Her grandmother played a role in bringing Emry back to reality when she began to spiral into a panic attack. Emry knew she could always rely on her grandmother to help her. Despite her fears, Emry worked at a local paint store selling paint to builders and individuals who were updating their homes or offices. She drove 45 minutes to Wichita every day to work. She was a good employee and top salesperson in the company. She was the glue which held the store together but was not compensated for the value she brought to the company. Her manager did not appreciate her and took advantage of her life circumstances. He knew she needed to work to support her grandmother and desperately wanted to advance in the company. He often reminded her he was the boss and responsible for providing job reviews to the CEO of the company. He used his power to create fear in Emry and used her as a puppet to his instruction. She was trapped and felt her hopes, and dreams hinged on her boss' arbitrary employee performance reviews which were often dependent upon his mood. He would share inappropriate things about his life and crossed the boundaries of an employee/boss relationship. He was angry with his wife because she did not spend enough time with him. He felt her job was interfering with his needs and her domestic responsibilities. This included, washing his clothes, running his errands, caring for the children, keeping the house clean, cooking dinner, and having sex with him at least five times a week. Emry did not feel comfortable listening to his stories and knew he was toxic. She felt dirty when he wanted to talk and avoided him as much as possible. She eventually quit her job after her boss asked her to meet him after work to discuss what she called, "A new job opportunity."

A Fairytale Gone Wrong – Alexa and Stephan

Alexa and Stephan grew up together in a small oil town just outside of Houston, Texas. They were good friends and found a unique trust in one another. They were not interested in sharing intimate time with one another, and they did not wish to have a commitment which kept them from dating other people. They went to the prom together, met each other for dinner on occasion, and took turns studying at one another's house. They were very close and considered themselves to be best friends. However, Alexa loved Stephan, but never told him. After graduation, Stephan took a scholarship to a college on the west coast and Alexa stayed in Texas to attend cosmetology school. They kept in contact with each other, but gradually stopped communicating when Alexa got pregnant by a young man she had been dating. He did not want to marry her and did not want the responsibility of a child. However, she was determined to have the child and work as an aesthetician. Alexa did this and discovered it was more difficult than she thought. It was challenging to work, pay for childcare, and living expenses. She was exhausted and felt as if she had no one. Eight years later, Stephan showed up and wanted to be a part of her life. He was working at a high paying job in Dallas. He was caring, loving, empathetic and not afraid to date a female who had a child. Alexa was happy Stephan was in her life again. However, two years had passed when Stephan started judging Alexa for staying home with her child instead of working. He would say, "It would be nice if you had some incentive to do something other than be a "Stay at home mom." He also often said, "You talk too much." "Sometimes it hurts my head to hear your voice." Little by little, Stephan the prince, became Stephen the Narcissist. But not really. He was always a narcissist. Money made him feel superior now and entitled to judge Alexa. Stephan saw an opportunity to take advantage of someone who was vulnerable and not be held accountable for his actions. Alexa had no power and could not control her situation. He made her feel inadequate, disempowered, anxious, and like a failure. Alexa is now working in the field of cosmetology. She and her daughter are building a life in Alabama.

Josephine and Roger

Josephine and Roger met at her place of employment. She was the director of a manufacturing plant and one of the few women who ever made it to that level in her company. She was committed and believed leadership begins at the bottom. She felt had it not been for those under her, she would not be the success she is today. Josephine knew her employees' strengths and understood what it took to build a team. She met Roger one day when he walked into the plant and asked for a job. He said, "He would do anything." He was a transplant from Arizona and explained he hoped to learn about the manufacturing business. He was well spoken, very convincing, and seemed to have passion. She explained he would begin as an entry level employee and work in the back warehouse loading and unloading boxes. He seemed to be fine with this and appreciated the chance to work. As time passed, he showed her he was committed to work hard and do the things necessary to prove his worth. Furthermore, he seemed to have fun and had a good rapport with the other employees. He was usually available to take on a second shift or fill in for someone who did not show or wanted to take a sick day. It became a joke in the plant that Roger was the "Savior." He was never far from being available to lend a helping hand. This showed in his compensation and promotion to manager. He frequently visited Josephine in her office to chat about the company and his goals. He was very serious about having Josephine's job title one day. She was flattered and took his desire to have her job lightly because she was retiring in the next two years. The relationship got personal the more time he spent in her office. He was charismatic, interested in her as a person, trustworthy, and driven to learn from her success. After hearing from a co-worker she was going thru a divorce, Roger dropped by her office more often and subtly integrated himself in her personal life. He was experienced at playing upon the emotions of others to secure a space in their life. He gracefully extracted her life story in all its joy and tragedy. It was not long before he made his way to the top of the company. He could not have done this without the support of Josephine. He also managed to move into Josephine's home. They were married after one year of living together. Josephine started losing herself to Roger's obsession with control and a superficial lifestyle. He began to spend money he did not have on cars, boats, parties, and girls. It was important for Roger to be perceived as wealthy, smart, and influential. He was a fraud and a conman in an Armani suit purchased with a maxed-out credit card. After ten years of marriage, Josephine lost everything. She was forced to file bankruptcy due to Roger's lying, cheating, stealing, and borrowing money from the bank to pay off his depts. She felt like a fool for believing Roger was honest. After the bankruptcy hearing, Roger filed for divorce. He left her with nothing. He went on to marry a woman whom he had been seeing throughout the course of their marriage.

THE NARCISSIST BULLY

Narcissist bullies are people who build themselves up by humiliating you or those around you. They will intentionally hurt you by using your past against you to emotionally sabotage any progress you may have made by healing. They will mock, exploit, threaten, and use your vulnerability to feel superior and control you or the situation. Gaslighting, intimidation, rejection, and different forms of abandonment are tactics used by the narcissist bully. In a nutshell, narcissistic bullying is any form of psychological or emotional abuse. Narcissist bullying is a catalyst to control you, gain power over you, and keep you emotionally submissive in the moment or relationship.

Jamie and Skyler

Skyler and Jamie met on an online dating site. Both were looking for a causal relationship. They were both retired and were seeking a companion who could travel. He was a retired engineer, and she was a widow. Jamie was eight years older than Skyler, but this was not an issue for either person. After three months of dating one another, they were compatible. Their first trip was to Colorado in the spring. Each enjoyed the mountains and liked to hike. Upon arriving, Jamie wanted to rest from the long drive. Skyler did not. He was eager to hike and seemed angry. He said, "We did not drive this far to take a nap." Jamie felt bad and was surprised by his mood. Jamie conceded and they went on a hike. They had a wonderful time, but when they returned, Skyler wanted to go to dinner immediately. She was hoping to shower, but he insisted. She grabbed her backpack, and they went to a small restaurant just outside of town. Jamie was questioning her decision to travel with Skyler and asked him if there was something wrong? He became defensive and attempted to blame her for his mood. Jamie apologized and tried to better understand what she did to make him so disappointed in the time they had spent together. She asked him for direction, was accused of not being empathetic to his feelings and stated how she should have known he wanted to hike upon arrival. She again apologized. The rest of the evening was silent, as Skyler was punishing her by abandoning the relationship while in the same space. Skyler was passive-aggressive the next day making it difficult for Jamie to determine if he wanted to reconcile or fight. Jaime asked him to please communicate with her so they could get back on a good track to have fun. He took this as if she was insinuating he was the problem and the reason they were not enjoying the trip. At this point Skyler mocked her, making her feel unwanted and not worthy of his relationship. Unfortunately, Jamie is still with Skyler and suffering from his narcissistic bullying and emotional control. There is hope, as she has not stopped trying to get help and help herself.

Jeffery and Alicia

Jeffery was an attorney at a prestigious law firm. He was charismatic, successful, and obnoxious. He was good at reading people, likable on the outside, but a bully behind closed doors. He was given the role of mentoring a female colleague to become a partner in his law firm. Her name was Alicia. She was more than qualified for advancement, had an outstanding reputation in the courtroom, and made a good example for women who were considering law as a profession. She was also the Chair on a Board supporting young women in leadership. Jeffery was known to make sexist comments and downplay success for women. He once said, "Careers are short lived for women because their emotions lead their decisions." Alicia would roll her eyes and felt sorry for him. She viewed his sexism as childish, showing his insecurity, and intimidation of her education and success. Her strength and unresponsiveness to his intimation made Jeffrey angry and more uneasy. Alicia refused to allow him to control her and would not placate to his need to have power and control over her. Jeffery stepped out of the position as a mentor to Alicia. It was a decision made by Jeffery. He was not successful at bullying Alicia and could not get his narcissist supply met through controlling her.

Dr. Courtney Linsenmeyer - O'Brien, Ph.D, MHR, PLC

Successful and independent people are not immediately interesting to the narcissist unless they are climbing a professional lifestyle to achieve status and success and need something the person has.

PERSONAL RELATIONSHIPS

Relationships are measured by the different degrees of efforts we put into them based upon the trust factors we have with the person. In other words, we place an emotional value on a relationship contingent upon the degree of trust we have for a person to have our heart. There is also sexual intimacy which when shared with another person whom we trust, can bring great satisfaction within the uniqueness of the relationship. The key word is, "Shared." Narcissists do not reciprocate love because they do not feel love on a vulnerable level. They want you to love and admire them for the greatness they possess and remind them of this every day. Because their self-love is so consuming, there is no room for shared intimacy. Just like Narcissus who fell in love with his own reflection until he went crazy, the Narcissist cannot see beyond himself. They prioritize power over intimacy. To maintain supremacy, they monopolize the direction of their personal relationships by playing emotional games. Arguing, verbal abuse, gaslighting, and passive aggressive comments like, "I would call more if I heard from you more often," or "I would like to have sex with you, but you never come to bed on time." How can you be in a relationship with someone who blocks emotional intimacy? You can, but it is a one-way journey structured to fulfill the needs of the narcissist. There is no emotional reciprocity.

Personality challenges represent a threat to the sustainability of the narcissist's well-groomed self-image. Independent views of those less likely to be manipulated re-route the narcissist's distorted perception of their self-importance. These people can oftentimes see through the narcissist's self-love whereas some are more easily fooled. The deception can be so well hidden, the narcissist's toxic reality of their existence is virtually unseen and disguised. Some narcissists are so proficient at manipulation that relationships often become a play write, one which is self-directed and produced in a manner which best allows him to be center stage. He is the star, director, and producer all in one. People are carefully chosen and crafted to fulfill the demands of his ego, and their roles shift accordingly. When other opinions or ideas are suggested, the situation can become overbearing and challenging to resolve. They do not go beyond themselves to try to understand another person and will overpower forms of reasoning. It feels like an attack. Any opportunity for resolve is dismissed or discounted. You may notice they are focused on the output of thought and discount any contributions you offer to achieve a fare and sound solution. They will also take bits and pieces of the person's words to use for better positioning and/or to achieve a given agenda. This can be very confusing.

Narcissists develop close relationships overtime that they can lead, influence, and ultimately convince of their greatness. They are the masterminds behind gathering relationships which endorse their perception of self and pledge to follow based upon the guidance of their mission. Attempting to gain control, the narcissist may withhold love, intimidate, or bribe you to attain control. Other tactics include ultimatums, overt dominance, fear, projecting superior intelligence, or playing a victim. They are masters at hiding behind their own fears and controlling their actions.

Many narcissists are accomplished at masking their agendas. Their disposition feels safe, secure, and gratifying. They are convincing and skilled at disguising their self-interests to conquer their agendas. Their charm and charisma are used to persuade you into agreement by abandoning your ideas or positions. If charm does not allure or convince you of the narcissist's superiority, more drastic measures may be used to achieve power. We see their behaviors accommodate the unique vulnerabilities of each relationship and executed differently depending upon the strengths and weaknesses of the person they are manipulating. All people are rivals until allegiance has been proven through validating their self-worth and compliance. Your unconditional devotion is a requirement to avoid conflict and punishment is inevitable if they question your loyalty. Your questionable commitment is a threat to the narcissist's ego and feelings of superiority. If challenged, the penalty can be severe or mild; this depends upon the overall situation and people involved; the stronger personality will be more difficult to win over than the person who avoids conflict. This brings to point the diverse ways in which the narcissist seeks control and power from all directions. The world is the narcissist's playground. The narcissist chooses their relationships. It is based upon their need for an endless supply of attention, affirmation, validation, and (most importantly), the degree to which you can be manipulated and controlled.

FEAR BOMBING VS LOVE BOMBING

<u>Fear bombing</u> is something narcissists will do in order to keep you close and make you feel as if you need them. This is mostly seen through the narcissist's ability to emotionally manipulate and control those close. Because most people are not consciously aware this manipulation is occurring, it goes undetected and may never be discovered until their victim is emotionally destroyed. More specifically, the victim often develops anxiety and other mental health disorders seen as serious thoughts and acts of suicide. Unfortunately, this turmoil invites further attempts to control and manipulate the victim.

<u>Love bombing</u> on the other hand, is overt manipulation which takes the form of gift giving, spontaneous calls during the day to

say, "I love you," and heart felt texts and acts of giving affection visible to others. Dr. Tina Swithin, Ph.D. states, "The recipient is bombarded with attention, which leaves little time for true contemplation and reflection," (2018, pg. 19). These behaviors are not done out of a genuine display of love or concern for other's wellbeing. It is designed to create a perception of love, commitment, greatness, and adoration. On a more intimate level, love bombing can occur to re-establish power which may have been lost somewhere in the relationship. Debbie Mirza, states, "Love bombing is where groundwork is laid for you to fully trust and believe in this person for years to come, (2017, pg. 24). It is also used in the event the narcissist feels there may be a chance they could be abandoned. They will do most anything to have attention and a constant supply of people around them. One person cannot meet the excessive amounts of ego supply needed to affirm the narcissist's self-worth. This is one reason it is impossible to have a committed love relationship with a narcissist.

True love does not call for obsessive amounts of attention, obscenely expensive gifts, or constant doting behaviors. There is something very wrong if a person is doing this to you. It can be flattering and make you feel special, but the intentions are derived from a toxic place. Know too these tactics are meant to be intoxicating and come with a price. You are expected to provide equal amounts of attention and adoration for the narcissist in return.

Know that the narcissist is leaving someone on the discard either now or sometime in the future when they have captured you. They cannot be alone and have someone on reserve or working on it.

SCRIPTING RELATIONSHIPS/CREATING THEIR OWN REALITY

A narcissist is always looking through you and at others for affirmation through your allegiance and ego protection. On a much larger scale, they will shape you into becoming something you are not. Everyone is viewed as an opportunity to enhance the narcissist's image and affirm the person who they believe themselves to be. Scripting relationships is done in a manipulative way and one in which you become a part of the narcissists fanaticized identity. They use you as a landscape to build an image of themselves. This is designed to reflect at them what they want to see in themselves.

If it is one thing you must know about a narcissist is they are always on the hunt.

A PATHOLOGICAL NARCISSIST

A Pathological Narcissist is someone who's in-love with an idealized self-image, which they project in order to avoid feeling (and being) their real, disenfranchised, wounded self. Deep down, most pathological narcissists feel weak and fearful, even if they painfully do not want to admit it. To cope with this personality, recognize that their emotional development is stunted and determine if they will get help. Most narcissists will not, as they are the author of their own story. They carefully create their own narrative, characters, and direct their life to feel safe, important, and account for predictability. Simply put, they see life and people as a landscape of opportunities to navigate their self-love.

Narcissists cannot objectively see their faults. They are blind to self-awareness, hence any effort to resolve conflict is a dead end. This means they exist in a world of irrational reality for which they are never obligated to own up to their mistakes. They see no reason to apologize for what they believe is not the cause of their actions. Therefore, they do not have remorse and lack the ability to have empathy for others whom they believe are wrong in the first place, and the cause of their own distress. The comment often used to deflect, and shift blame onto others is, "I'm sorry you feel that way." It may sound empathetic and feel like a segway into resolution but is not! This comment is a crafty way to construct words which ultimately say, "It is your fault, and your feelings do not matter." This does not help achieve a resolution in which two people work to become more aware and accountable for their faults. Because of this, the narcissist has no internal compass guiding ration and applicable resolution to conflict.

DISTORTED THOUGHTS OF INTIMACY AND COMMITMENT.

How do you fulfill sexual fantasies and intimacy within a committed relationship without betraying the emotional and physical commitment? This is difficult, but possible if desires and feelings are not left to resolve themselves. Interpretation, fear and assumptions will mislead the relationship and dissolve opportunities to explore fulfillment. If thoughts and desires are not revealed, it is unlikely both people ever fully understand the needs unique to one another. This passage is both encouraging and is a warning before getting emotionally and sexually involved with a narcissist. The narcissist is not emotionally invested in the feelings or needs of others. Therefore, the sexual relationship is seen as an opportunity to navigate their own sexual desires. This is dangerous, as it is impossible to experience healthy intimacy with a person who is self-focused on the outcome of their own desires. Using commitment to shape the journey and mold an outcome which meets the needs of only one person is *wrong* and can be toxic to the overall relationship. If both people do not share the same goals or intimate expectations, the satisfaction within their intimate lives will likely be unsuccessful. If one person must convince the other to engage in sexual acts not mutually agreed upon, both should reconsider activities. Commitment to another is not based upon conforming to the desires of another. However, narcissists can be creative in their methods to achieve self-satisfaction by using their partner as the main tool. An example is a man who looks at swinging to help cope with anxieties related to his erectile issues. Driven by a fear of confronting a complete loss of his sexual veracity, the man almost convinces his wife that sharing sexual experiences with others would be good for their marriage. His approach was unique in that he explained how this would give her opportunities to explore any unconscious thoughts she may have regarding sex and feel sexual in ways she never knew she could. "Just watching" or "Just knowing" she was enjoying herself would be enough to satisfy him and make him feel accomplished as a successful sexual provider. He even attempted to justify how this would make the marriage stronger and maybe help fix his erectile problem. To him, this was a mutually beneficial solution.

ONLINE SEXUAL BEHAVIORS AND THE NARCISSIST

Now more than ever, infidelity is as close as a screen swipe, text, or hidden conversation inside of social media. It is easier to hide, more accessible, and (more times than not) can become addictive. Because sexual betrayal is within reach at any time of day or night, the behavior is amplified and the fear of getting caught is less of a concern. Risks are taken in which people will bring their behavior into personal spaces which should remain sacred to the spouse. This means cheating is brought into a couple's bedroom, bathroom, and even children's spaces unknown to their spouse. Nothing becomes off limits when deceit is so easy to hide. This is a narcissist's playground. Its landscape provides easy access to those vulnerable to manipulation, sexual escapades, and relationships which require no commitment or emotional reciprocity. Dr. Lowen, MD says it best, "Narcissists have a fear of intimacy because it requires an exposure of the self. One cannot be intimate and hide behind a mask or image. But physical closeness makes no such demand and can be used to hide self and feelings. Narcissists may use sexual closeness to avoid true intimacy, for the darkness and the proximity are obstacles to seeing the other person." He goes on to say, "As a result, sex becomes a mechanical act between two bodies while the feelings are aroused by and focused on fantasy partners," (1997, pg.123). The narcissist sees the online cultural shifts of sexual opportunity as just that—opportunity. Because the narcissist views people as transactions, infidelity is a game. Sex and the internet are another avenue used to navigate self-love and deceit.

Can you have a fulfilling sexual relationship with someone who is emotionally unavailable? You can, but it is toxic, and you will likely end up trapped in a co-dependent relationship where abuse feels like love.

USING SEX TO CONTROL

Narcissists often have a heightened sense of sexuality and view sex very differently than other people do. They see sexuality more in terms of power, and an opportunity to emotionally control a partner. They prey upon people who are emotionally vulnerable, easily influenced, looking to exit a bad situation, and likely to idolize them. There is a promise to love the person in ways they have never been loved. This creates higher levels of trust and emotional availability to occur. These feelings find their way into the bedroom where emotional transparency is likely to be at its highest, (e.g., sharing time together after a sexual experience). Self-disclosure is then used as a weapon to control. The narcissist is seeking to capitalize on opportunities to control, and sex is a common way in which power can be yielded. Even when they are in a committed relationship, they are on the lookout for other partners who can give them the attention they feel they deserve. This is because more than one partner enhances their internal self-image. If one partner is not fulfilling, the narcissist will move onto the next person who will. This continues to validate their sense of importance and gives them options to fulfill their endless need to control.

PROJECTING: THE DANGEROUS RELATIONSHIP

Projecting is related to taking unwanted emotions a person doesn't like about themselves and assigning them to another person. This is important to know if you are living with or are close to a narcissist. Narcissists will project their self-hate upon others to disassociate with their own self-loathing. They do this to avoid looking inside of themselves to address their own fears, insecurities, and feelings of inferiority. They aren't telling you "Your" story, they are telling you, their story. Projecting negativity onto someone else immediately shifts blame and makes it appear as if they are not the reason for the conflict. By default, (and in their eyes), you are the cause of the dispute or problem. Common phrases used are: "If you would accept that you are the cause of our problems, we might have a chance." "You are the liar." "You never said that" (knowing that you did), and "You don't have the ability to give me what I need." Try to understand they are not talking about you. They are projecting themselves onto you to subdue their feelings, deflect attention away from themselves, and assign blame to you for their actions.

Narcissism can be outwardly identified. This may be the person who seeks approval through expensive cars, a flashy lifestyle, and other outward appearances. However, there are many narcissists who can only be identified from the inside of a relationship. They are skilled at using projection as a tool to manipulate and control others. This can be seen through a tactic known as Gaslighting, in which confusion is created and used to make you question your own reality. Note, this is emotional abuse. This narcissist suffers a fear of abandonment, low self-esteem, and secretly feels disempowered when around others who trigger feelings of inferiority. Controlling people gives the narcissist a sense of security and is likely to instill a false belief that others need the narcissist.

Try to recognize you are listening to the wrong voice! Know the difference between someone who is using you to avoid accountability verses someone who is emotionally stable. If you believe you are, or could be a victim of emotional manipulation, find professional help. Remove yourself from the situation before you start believing you are the person whom the narcissist is projecting onto you—Themselves.

INSANTIY AND GASLIGHTING

"Gaslighting" is a 1944 psychological thriller film, about a woman whose husband slowly manipulates her into believing that she is going insane. In the movie, (and in reality) gaslighting is used to describe a narcissist's abusive behavior, specifically when he manipulates reality in such a way as to make his wife feel unstable, and dependent on his control. This technique is used by a skilled emotional abuser who knows the power of fear and emotional control. The narcissist is no stranger to gaslighting. His keen ability to read people can be lethal and emotionally paralyze the victim.

The goal for the "Gaslighter" is to make their victim question their own judgement and diminish their self-worth, hence tricking the victim into being dependent on the narcissist. The manipulation occurs over a long period of time so his victim is less likely to feel the effects of being brainwashed. Timing is everything. The more time he spends placing his victim under the microscope, the better he understands how to play to their weakness.

It can start with seemingly inconsequential physical things – such as the abuser moving an item you put down, and suggesting you misplaced it. Furthermore, you find it later in a place which makes no sense and causes questions to arise concerning memory loss or the possibility of a brain disorder. An example would be finding your hairbrush in the washing machine or your car keys in the refrigerator. This may then escalate to flat-out lying about events. They might deny things you know they said or claim things like emotional or verbal abuse never occurred. This can ultimately make you feel as if you are crazy. The goal at this point in the game is to make you genuinely believe you are going insane, ultimately eroding away at the difference between what is real and in your own head. Gaslighting eventually isolates the victim into a state of crippling fear. This alienates the victim from their support systems and prevents them from escaping the abuse they are suffering. When it is all said and done, you feel as if you have been in a car crash with a professional race car driver who intended to wreck the car without completely totaling its parts. You leave the scene confused, beat up by the impact and severity of the incident and worse, you don't necessarily trust your immediate recall as to how it all happened. What's more, you are made to believe the wreck was your fault. By the time it is all over, you leave the scene questioning your reality and wondering what you could have done differently to prevent the catastrophic collision. This kind of confusion is the narcissist's ability to reduce the victim's ability to think critically and independently. Once this happens, the narcissist can convince you of a reality which is not true, justify their actions, conquer a situation, and seed unwanted thoughts.

A MINDFUCK

What comes to your mind when you see the words, "Mind" and "Fuck" used in conjunction? Confusion, distortion, danger, hesitation, or impairment? If we had to use one emotion to describe all the words, it would most likely be, "Fear." Mindfuck is slang for an experience which creates disturbing emotions, such as confusion, fear, and a mixture of other uncomfortable emotions which are psychologically damaging. It is deeply distressing, and a tactic used by narcissists, abusive leaders, and sociopaths. It seriously interferes with an individual's ability to think on their feet, keep their thoughts in order, or verbally defend themselves. It ultimately suspends an individual's ability to stay connected to a stream of consciousness while in an argument or simple conversation. You begin to feel lost and experience an overall sense of helplessness. Feeling ignorant and stupid is also common. Furthermore, the person cannot cope because the narcissist is diminishing their self-esteem, and self-confidence, by fostering an overall sense of defeat. The strategy is to destabilize your emotions through various methods of communication:

1. Verbal attacks which sabotage mental processing. This creates emotional confusion and often impairs thinking.
2. Non-verbal behavior such as rolling their eyes while you are talking to them. This is patronizing and designed to elevate the narcissist's ego while positioning them in a place of superiority. It comes from the idea of self-importance and arrogance.

3. Disconnecting from the interaction, making you feel insignificant and later, ask "Why did you alienate our conversation?" "You always make me feel bad about myself."
4. Degrading comments such as, "You never can remember how it all happened." This makes the person feel doubtful and weak.
5. Making passive-aggressive comments such as, "I am not the one who is mad," or "Fine, whatever!" This incites conflict, hence circumventing healthy resolution.
6. Making statements like, "That is irrelevant." This makes a person actually "Feel" irrelevant.
7. "I like that dress on you, but for some reason, I liked it better when you bought it." This is a backhanded compliment meant to make the person question their body image, or ask themselves, "What's wrong with me now?"
8. Accuse you of cheating because they claim you talk about the affair in your sleep.
9. Ask you to do things you do not feel comfortable doing and use your love for them as leverage to get what they want and later say, "I did not make you do anything."
10. Talk "At" you instead of to you. This is meant to disempower you and show you that you do not matter.

This is not a complete overview of mind manipulation. However, all the above examples are how a narcissist will intentionally start an argument to deflect from something they have done wrong and control the way you feel about yourself. Emotional control is used to dominate the dynamic of the interaction. Once this occurs, the narcissist can quickly redirect blame through emotional and psychological manipulation. The following is an example:

Steve and His Wife

Steve was caught by his wife having an affair with an intern at the hospital where he worked as a surgeon. His wife suspected it, and her suspicions were confirmed by a nurse who worked at the same hospital. The nurse had witnessed Steve's sexualized behavior over the years with young women who were vulnerable to his charm. The nurse contacted and met with his wife one day at a nearby coffee shop and disclosed Steve's adulterous behavior over a 10-year period. She eventually confronted Steve when she had proof he had been unfaithful and was still cheating. He panicked after learning he had been exploited by the nurse. His wife left their home to stay with a friend in Florida. Steve called her and after three days, she decided to come home and listen to his story. However, there was no discussion. He immediately began to chastise her because she went behind his back to learn he was having an affair. He said, "If you did not trust me, why did you marry me?" "If you cared about me, you would understand why I did this." Steve determined her phantom distrust in him created an emotional separation in bed and therefore he had to cheat. Steve did not let her speak. He yelled, asked her questions without giving her a chance to answer, and then answered the questions he asked her. He accused her of cheating and then called her a hypocrite. All of this was happening at once and Steve's wife was confused and mentally exhausted from trying to make sense of it all. This is what it is like to be a victim of a narcissist's Mindfuck theatrics. They avoid taking responsibility for their behaviors by diverting their actions onto others in an aggressive way which pathologizes you and psychologically defeats you. By being on the offense they automatically place themselves in a position of power. You are left to defend yourself in an unexpected situation of escalating chaos. The intent is to violate your emotional and psychological stability, using any tactic to confuse, intimidate, and force you into submitting to believe their false reality.

CHAPTER 2

DROWNING IN YOUR OWN BLOOD!

Narcissists enjoy going to battle. In fact, they will intentionally instigate conflict to remind others of their superiority and entitlement within a relationship. A method used to create outright domination and a feeling of desperation in their victim is called Offensive Fighting. The strategy is used to, "Beat you to the punch." It begins as a passive form of verbal manipulation in which the narcissist questions and twists your words into lies. He or she may say things like, "Are you sure you said that?" or "You just don't remember." He will also tell you how you "really" feel and think. This is a stall tactic used so you will get caught up in defending yourself while they reposition to verbally assault, belittle, or make you feel as though you are losing your mind. The mode of operation unfolds like this: "You are so stupid," "Your career is a joke," "You just don't remember what you said – I think you might be losing your memory." At this point, you feel as if they are doing brain surgery on you while you are awake, watching, and drowning in your own blood.

EMOTIONAL PARALYSIS

Feeling helpless, traumatized, and unable to move forward with life is how one feels after escaping the emotional abuse of a narcissist. It is difficult to explain how the wounds destroy esteem, self-confidence, and the ability to move through life. The narcissist treats those close as if it is their responsibility to make them happy and appear special to others. They are only as good as others can make them look good and add to their self-view of superiority. If those around the narcissist fail to do this, they are overlooked and discarded.

EPISODIC ERRUPTIONS

Mood swings are a common characteristic in the narcissist's personality. Their inability to regulate their emotions in appropriate ways or take criticism can trigger rage or shift of mood in an instant. Dr. Hollman, Ph.D. (2020, pg. 11) states, "They have difficulty when things do not go their way, and they will be hard-pressed to ever admit fault when they are wrong, which makes it hard for them to take any kind of criticism, even if it is constructive." She goes on to say, "They may react to criticism with outbursts of disparaging others ruthlessly, yelling, crying, and denigrating others who are close to them and care about them." These fits are often unpredictable and dangerous if you happen to be in their way. You may be in the middle of what seems to be a pleasant conversation but, caught off guard by a sudden change in their emotional response. Or you may find you are defending yourself from one of their random outbursts while trying to make sense of it, as it is occurring. An example follows:

Blake and Gabriella

Blake and Gabriella were married for five years when Gabriella noticed occasional mood shifts during simple disagreements. Blake was triggered by things that never seemed to be issues in the beginning of their relationship. His anger would escalate and without resolution afterwards, he would act as though nothing occurred. It was as if the anger never occurred. This was confusing and emotionally exhausting for Gabriella. Because there was no grounded emotion within the moment, it was difficult to understand who she was talking to. "He was yelling at me because the dishes were still in the sink and saying my career was interfering with my responsibilities as a wife." He left the room only to come back and ask me what I wanted for dinner and if I wanted to go to the Home and Garden show this weekend." Nothing is more important to the narcissist than what their current thoughts are within the moment, and it is your fault if you do not understand their intentions. Blake felt justified in his attack on Gabbi because he saw Gabbi as someone who owed him acts of service in exchange for the material things he provided for her. Leaving the room after the attack was normal, as was returning five minutes later as if the interaction never happened. The narcissist's reality operates on its own only to receive input which accommodates their emotion and motive at the time needed.

COVERT VS OVERT NARCISSISTS

Both covert and overt narcissists crave attention, control, and use others around them to make them feel better about themselves. Covert narcissists tend to be very sensitive and take things personal which are not intended to hurt them or directed to them. They may dismiss others by leaving the room during a conversation, roll their eyes or avoid making eye contact while someone is talking to them, or completely withdraw socially where participation is needed. Covert narcissists show disrespect and apathy towards others because they do not see a need to interact unless there is something in it for them. People are interesting and have a purpose if there is something to gain. They often surround themselves with "Yes" people and anyone who will listen to their ideas. They are, "Quick to rescue and eager to find solutions to all your problems," (Behary, 2013, pg. 28). This strokes their ego, (providing them with a feeling of importance), and gives them an avenue to control in a furtive or unseen way. They are also strategic, cunning, lack empathy, and emotionally and psychologically abusive. People only exist for the covert narcissist to create the image they see themselves to be. They are very intuitive, calculating, and will stop at nothing to get what they want and hurt you if you get in their way. Perhaps the most disturbing thing about a covert narcissist is they have a following who believes them to be savior like, honest, loving, and mentally sound.

Overt narcissists are like coverts in their need for others when it best suits their need or agenda. The overt narcissist is more outward in their efforts to achieve their agenda. If they do not get what they want, the overt narcissists can become aggressive in their tone, attitude, and behaviors. Achieving their agenda is more, "Hands on" and more visible. They seek approval by outwardly appearing to be successful, wealthy, likable, and powerful. This plays into their feelings of entitlement and superiority above others. Overt narcissists also find power in exploiting others. This can be a vehicle to control others through an eventual breakdown of self-esteem and self-confidence. Lastly, where a convert plays upon others sympathy to gain attention and control others, an overt narcissist takes an active approach to control by outward measures of control. They are also keen at emotional manipulation to control. They can calculate how to get up into your business slowly by using both covert and overt manipulation. This book is mostly about the narcissist who is skilled to use both forms in unison and independent of the other. This is the most dangerous form of manipulation, and the impact of control comes from all directions.

I will again state it is unlikely and perhaps impossible to reform a narcissist. They do not change. Healthy living is contingent upon one's ability to dodge narcissistic people or get obliterated by their recklessness and agendas. However, one must recognize this in order to take cover. One day when my (at the time) 8-year-old son and I were on a walk, he said he, "Wanted to see the oncoming cars" as we walked. I asked, "Why?" His response was, "Because if I'm going to die, I want to see it coming." I thought, well of course you would want to see it coming ....so you might have a chance to live. I laughed and thought this was clever. He was thinking on a much higher level for an 8-year-old. It was so true though. You should do your best in any circumstance to protect yourself in the moment to maximize your safety in the future. My son is still brilliant.

Justine's Story

One Saturday morning, I was at the gym on the treadmill and looked down at my phone to discover I had 10 missed calls from the same number. There were no voice mail messages, but there was one text from this unidentified number. The text read, "Please call me as soon as possible. If you are taking new clients, I need to schedule an appointment with you." "I am sorry to bother you on a weekend, but I am desperate for help. Thank you." I reached out to Justine later but was unable to make the connection. I later learned this was because Justine's boyfriend learned she was seeking help for issues she was having with their relationship. He found her journal which she wrote in daily to help her collect her thoughts and manage her anxiety. Justine had drawn pictures of broken hearts and eyes on the back cover of the journal. She had written, "My heart hurts and I cannot see a future with the one I am with." "God please help me." When I heard her voice, I knew she was suffering at the time she left her message.

I HATE YOU DON'T LEAVE ME!

If you know you are living with a narcissist, you are aware of the different methods of emotional manipulation and the confusion it brings to your life. One day you may feel as if you are loved, safe, and with the right person. They are attentive, respectful, engaged in your feelings, and appear to be actively working on things to promote positive outcomes within your relationship. This provides hope which motivates and inspires us to stay in a relationship because hope indicates a "Chance" things will get better. The truth of the matter is, your relationship with the narcissist may seem to be headed towards a brighter and healthier reality, but most of the time this is an unhealthy cycle which never gets farther than one's hope. The possibility the narcissist will change gets lost within a co-dependent relationship. Both people justify staying in the relationship and enable the other to do those things which keep the toxic elements sustaining their interactions. The longer this continues, feelings of desperation guide the overall trajectory of the relationship. No one likes to feel without options or as if they are trapped. This creates resentment, fear, and frustration; especially if there is still hope. Because of the confusion, cognitive dissonance may occur, and incongruent feelings collide creating an overwhelming sense of anxiety. "I hate you, don't leave me" says it best.

YOU SAY THAT YOU LOVE ME BUT DO NOT SHOW IT

Narcissists try hard to make you feel you are not showing them enough love or working hard enough in the relationship to make them happy. Enough is never enough and the affirmations you offer do not satisfy their narcissist supply. They measure a successful relationship by how much time you spend with them and away from others. Your allegiance to fulfilling their toxic love ideal is exhausting and impossible because in either case, your fulltime job is to convince them your purpose is to validate their identity through their distorted ideas of commitment and their self-perception. They will shame you into spending time with them and guilt you into believing you are the cause of any relationship issue.

Narcissists are not comfortable with your independence because there is always a fear you will become interested in someone or something outside of them. They get jealous easily and take it personal if you have close relationships. Any time spent with someone else is time taken away from the attention you could be giving them.

THINGS A NARCISSIST FEARS MOST

A. <u>Other's emotional expectations</u> – Narcissists fear being asked to reciprocate what would naturally be expected within their inner psyche. It explains why they push back when others ask for their love. There is fear in a healthy committed relationship. Trust, honesty, integrity, love, and shared intimacy are all values the narcissist lacks but are good at pretending to hone. Eventually, their apathy is discovered through their disinterest in reciprocity and/or deceitful actions of different forms of betrayal. One of the most obvious reasons they are fearful of emotional expectations is it represents a loss of power and control.

B. <u>Themselves</u> – The underlying theme of a narcissist is a feeling of self-loathing and not feeling good enough. Therefore, they work hard to appear as someone they are not. Insecurity is masked through a projected image of someone who is confident, kind, successful, and someone who others want to be like. A lifetime of living inside of this false reality becomes their reality. They fear looking into themselves to see the person for who they truly are. The real person is weak, fears abandonment, and lies to get others to like or want to be with them.

C. <u>Abandonment</u> – Many narcissists have suffered great wounds during childhood symptomatic of abuse and abandonment from a primary attachment figure. Therefore, it makes sense their massive fear of desertion is also an impetus to control things and people around them. Control allows them to feel in charge of the emotional direction of the relationship, and if there is trouble in paradise, it is better to be the one who leaves, than be the one who is left behind.

D. <u>Being alone</u> – Being alone is different from abandonment, but similar in that they intuit rejection. The narcissist fears both, but the two are vastly different in nature; being able to sit with yourself and being alone to measure psychological fitness and mental stability. It also gives you a measuring stick for who and what you will allow in your life. Being alone can provide you with personal insight, embrace your value, help you heal from pain, and learn from mistakes. Moreover, sitting with yourself can provide healthy directional change through spiritual awareness. Unless you are a narcissist, surrendering to a form of spirituality is significant to emotional and psychological wellbeing. It is a valuable tool with which to gauge your emotional availability and comfort level in being alone in silence. Ideally, we would all push forward to find more internal peace and be closer to feelings of tranquility. The good thing is most people do want to try and become better versions of themselves. However, the narcissist thinks he is the best version of himself factoring in his own criteria and leaving out his own reality.

I am not denying these things can be intimidating, nor am I implying that if you cannot sit alone with yourself you are a narcissist. There is a difference between being open to personal growth and building a world in which control and manipulation are used to avoid self-scrutiny. The narcissist does the latter because they are terrified of being authentic for fear others will leave them. Therefore, they manipulate others to avoid being alone.

E. <u>Rejection</u> – Rejection can bring a narcissist to their knees, trigger rage, or cause them to seek revenge on the person who has rejected them. The different reactions are contingent upon the person(s) involved and the situation. For instance, if rejection is experienced with a spouse, the reaction can spin into emotional manipulation channeled through verbal abuse or subtle behaviors which leave bad feelings lingering around the spouse. Better to be the rejecter than the one who suffers rejection.

F. <u>Loss of power and control</u> – Dr. Lowen, MD, (1997, pg. 84) states, "Power is a way to protect oneself against humiliation. It is a means of overcoming a feeling of inferiority." I believe this is taken to the extreme with the narcissist. Having a superior position over others, (be it personal or professional), is at the essence of a narcissist's insecurities and their ability to survive. Without it, they will panic and do everything they can to recover a position of control. This is because they fear their own vulnerability and do not have the confidence to share a collaborative relationship with anyone. Therefore, the narcissist's relationships exist solely on a hierarchy of control. I will call this for what it is: Dominance. They are always seeking a life of dominance to gain power and avoid loss of control.

G. <u>Criticism</u> – It never feels good to learn someone has criticized you. However, most people can recover from criticism without suffering lifelong effects. Furthermore, most have the capacity to "consider the source" through some form of deductive reasoning and move on down the road. This is not the case for the narcissist. It is not possible for them to process the difference between constructive vs destructive criticism, much less hang in there when someone doesn't think before they speak. The narcissist feels criticized when people disagree, challenge, or question his decisions. Therefore, he becomes offended, acts entitled, and feels rejected. This may sound like the behaviors a child might exhibit; this is because you are dealing with an adult child. Upon feeling judged, the narcissist reverts to a wounded child's psyche where attachment and safety issues ensued as a result of perceived environmental threats. This is known as the "Narcissist's Narcissistic Injury" which can be viewed as over-identifying with fear and mistrust. Simply put, the injured narcissist is reacting as the child he was when wounded or neglected by their primary caregiver.

H. <u>Being ignored</u> – Being ignored is cutting off a narcissist's supply; as far as he is concerned, others are supposed to adore, worship, and reaffirm his superiority, through affirmations.

For the narcissist, being overlooked or discounted feels like neglect and rejection. This is because, when he looks outside, he sees a world which owes him attention in return for his perceived greatness. Ignoring him is the equivalent to leaving him to be alone. What is more, being ignored could lead to being forgotten, and even worse, becoming invisible. This would be the death of his perceived, self-endowed image and accordingly, he would have no purpose without the adoration and approval of others. It is never about the intrinsic value of people and relationships.

I. <u>Being forgotten</u> – Being forgotten is like being ignored, only worse. Being ignored feels temporary because the things and people who take the place of the narcissist are only viewed as substitutions. According to the narcissist, there is still hope, to regain attention and once more, become the focus. Being forgotten means others have moved on to other things and people. Therefore, he has been replaced. This is the ultimate form of rejection because others should see his value and put him first. After all, when he is REPLACED, a narcissist feels they are no longer important.

J. <u>Being Invisible</u> – There are some people who prefer to melt into the woodwork and others who are content making an occasional appearance to the surface. Most of us fall into one of these two categories. There are elements which differentiate us from one another such as personality, flare, identity and so on. For the most part though, our attention seeking monitors are dialed down on a day-to-day basis. And then……there is the narcissist who needs to be viewed or thought of as being special, out of the ordinary, or unique in some way. These are the people you see out dining in a restaurant dominating the conversation, laughing unusually loud, or making a scene because their food was cold. To put another spin on it, this could be the well-groomed individual who uses posturing to get his way, a kind of silent intimidation. Instead of yelling and screaming his food was cold, he will ask for the restaurant owner's name and want to know when he/she will be at their restaurant. Either way, you are supposed to look, watch, and listen to their production. This is the point in either example. The latter case is a passive way of asking for attention and the former case is a direct demand for attention and perhaps even gets a "I wonder who HE is?" as if the narcissist is someone special.

K. <u>Being exposed for who they are</u> – The narcissist is terrified others will discover the true nature of his wounded, and fragile ego. That underneath the many masks of success and adoration, he is helplessly dependent upon others to create his false identity of independence and stability in order to survive. In short, his projected self-presentation is a lie. Everything and everyone are an opportunity used to craft his perceived self-image and fulfill a desperate need for adoration. Furthermore, it is likely his relationships and successes were built on the backs of those he wounded, bullied, cheated, and pretended to like. Depending upon the skill level of his ability to manipulate, these individuals probably never felt a thing. Hence, they may not know they were victims of his evil and hidden agendas. His thought on this is, "You don't know what you don't know." Exposure is devastating to the narcissist; not because he feels remorse. He is upset at himself because he "messed up" somewhere along the way, risking exposure, rejection, and embarrassment.

L. <u>Embarrassment</u> – Although embarrassment makes us want to run and hide at times and can cause temporary physiological changes, (such as increased heart rate or blushing), the feeling usually subsides and gets properly processed in our brains. However, embarrassment to the narcissist feels like exploitation and humiliation. They do not digest the feelings of embarrassment in the same ways most of us do, because their wounded self is always working to protect itself from being seen as anything but secure. Narcissists hate being viewed as anything but perfect and righteous.

M. Strength and courage in others – Narcissists gravitate to people they can manipulate and control. Therefore, they choose those who are situationally down on themselves, or likely to let someone swoop in and rescue them. Ultimately, they choose those who are vulnerable and easy to control.

N. Successful people – The narcissist views your successes as a threat. Accomplishments, degrees, awards, and recognition all factor into the insecurities which challenge their overall perception of greatness. Although the narcissist may be successful by virtue of their own accomplishments, they are still intimidated by your achievements. This is because the narcissist is always looking to be the best and most admired person in the room.

They are also likely to be nervous around those who are of similar status and highly achievement oriented. This is complicated because they have a deep need for approval, affirmation, and acceptance, but are terrified of rejection amongst their peers. This is conflicting to their ego because they have a deep need for approval, acceptance, and desire to belong. Your success threatens their self-made views of interpersonal dominance and superiority. A very simple example of this is someone needing to reschedule a lunch meeting or date night. Instead of understanding the person's conflict in scheduling, the narcissist feels angered and entitled. In their mind, their time is more important than yours and adjusting their schedule to meet the needs of yours is imposing on their time and inconvenient.

O. <u>Your family and friends</u> – They are threatened by any support system and afraid those close will see them for who and what they are. Additionally, you are competition to the narcissist's obsessive desire for undivided attention. The saying, "Blood is thicker than water," has true meaning for most of us. The narcissist views family support systems as a threat, unless alliances have already strategically been put into place, in the event conflict might expose them, threaten their reputation, or cost them relationships. Additionally, family and friends are competition for the narcissist's desire to have your undivided attention.

P. <u>Emotionally intelligent people</u> – Emotional intelligence is the ability to identify, process, and understand one's emotions, independent of external stimuli or other's agenda. These people are highly intuitive, socially aware, have healthy boundaries, and embrace a high self-esteem. They also possess a high degree of self-awareness and hone natural instincts. Hence, it is much harder for the narcissist to manipulate these individuals because they are high functioning and can intuit inauthenticity. Meaning, they can read between the lines. The narcissist can quickly assess who he can or cannot fool. Therefore, you are unlikely to see a narcissist in therapy unless they stand to lose something such as a spouse or job. Otherwise, they may act indignant and say things like: "This is your problem, not mine," "I don't need therapy, you do," "I don't trust therapists," or "Only weak people go to therapy." Therapy challenges their ability to be accountable for their behavior and more importantly, be self-reflective; this is extremely hard, as they do not have the capacity, (or desire) to explore self-awareness.

A MASS OF SELF-DOUBT

The narcissist is a master at projecting self-confidence and success. However, these behaviors are an over exaggeration of emotional security and self-assuredness. In fact, turned inside-out, the façade is a reaction to the mass of self-doubt and insecurities they keep hidden from others. Their day-to-day reality is centered around two extraordinarily strong forces in which opposing elements of ego strength compete for a position of power. For example, when a narcissist's childlike needs are threatened by feelings of fear, insecurities, or low self-confidence, his alter personality shows up with a vengeance to rescue the child within from influences like rejection, judgment, and perceptions of failure. Narcissists despise what they know to be weaknesses within themselves. Therefore, instead of owning those weaknesses, they deny the weaknesses and attribute it to others. This is called "Projection," in which the ego defends itself against unconscious impulses, thoughts, or feelings by denying the weaknesses existence and transferring them onto others. "The narcissist's fears or actions become projected onto their victims and altered into the victim's wrongdoing rather than the Narcissist's," (Shahida, 2019, pg. 164). An example of this is Tory and Breanna's relationship.

Tory and Breanna met while working at a restaurant on the West Coast. Breanna moved from a small town just outside of Tulsa, Oklahoma to see if she could live on her own and attend college in a place far from Oklahoma. She would be the first to move away from her family and the only person who would have an education greater than a high school degree. She knew it would be difficult to not have her mother and father close, but she had a vision to experience life as she saw it in her dreams. Tory was a local and had worked at the restaurant from the time of turning 16 years old. She quickly noticed Breanna and they soon became friends. They shared time together outside of work and eventually learned they were physically and emotionally attracted to one another. Tory had an apartment not far from the restaurant, and Breanna was staying at a friend's until she could afford to live on her own. As time passed and they became committed to one another, Tory invited Breanna to move into her place. They would save money, share a car, and have more time with one another. It seemed to make sense. Breanna moved in, felt good about the decision, and was able to save her own money to go to college. She was excited and, on a journey to make her parents proud. After a hectic process of applying to three schools, she was accepted to two of the schools and offered a scholarship in which, her only expense would be the cost of her books if she maintained a 3.5 grade average. This was exciting and beyond what she imagined could happen to a poor girl from Oklahoma. Breanna called Tory after learning of the good news. It did not seem Tory was happy about Breanna's opportunity to attend college. It almost seemed as if Tory was angry. Breanna did not give this a second thought, as she was excited about going to school. As the semester began, Tory made comments to Breanna which made her wonder if she was misunderstanding the meaning behind what Tory way saying. This continued until Tory lost her temper with Breanna and began to make Breanna feel guilty about taking the scholarship. She would make hurtful comments which made Breanna doubt herself. Comments such as, "Are you sure that you want to pursue those classes next year?" "Do you really think a degree will make a difference in your future?" "Will you be able to support yourself if we ended our relationship right now?" These questions were used to destabilize Breanna's decision to pursue her academic goals. Tory was also projecting her own insecurities onto Breanna by attempting to make her feel as if she was not good enough, obligated to stay with Breanna, and question the value of her educational goals.

THE RAGE AND MASSACRE

Narcissistic rage is a psychological construct which describes a reaction to narcissistic injury, which is conceptualized as a perceived threat to his or her self-esteem or perceived self-identity. Narcissistic injury is a cause of distress and can lead to dysregulation of behaviors, (e.g., rage). Once triggered, there is nothing you can do to stop the force. The narcissist feels as if they have been victimized, so their natural reaction is to take hostages and make them victims. This is where rage is inflicted upon another person. The wreckage left behind after an episodic rage is disastrous and emotionally crippling. The recovery is painful and may be a lifelong journey depending upon the length of time you have been with the narcissist wounds as a result of trauma caused by verbal assaults and emotional abuse. If you have lived through a narcissist's attack, you understand what it is like to be taken to the "Dark Side" of their psyche.

Although you cannot stop the rage from occurring, you can prevent a massacre from happening. Think of this as taming a beast by subduing its force. Because the narcissist's rage is triggered by irrational fears and a threat to their self-worth, you must work within their construct in a non-threatening way. Ideally, you want to avoid injury to their self-view and self-esteem to prevent the rage episode from occurring at all. However, this is impossible because: a) you cannot always be the source of his narcissistic supply; b) walking on eggshells all the time is mentally and emotionally exhausting; c) it is not always possible to predict what will trigger their ego-injury.

Therefore, your initiative is to de-escalate their distress before it turns into weaponry used on you during their fit of rage. Self-preservation is your goal. Here are some tools you can use to diffuse a narcissist's rage:

- Don't buy a ticket to the fight.
- Don't argue.
- Use non-threatening language such as, "I understand," "That makes sense," "What do you think we should do?"
- Ask them questions about themselves.
- Never blame.
- Communicate using the words, "We," "Us," and "Our," instead of "You" or "I."
- Compliment them.
- Use a non-threatening tone of voice. This has a significant calming effect.
- Show empathy and concern in the moment and recognize it will not be reciprocated.
- Be the adult. This goes without saying.
- Forgive them, but do not say, "I forgive you." The narcissist will interpret this as a passive-aggressive statement placing blame onto them. You will not succeed at explaining the meaning behind your forgiveness.

If you are living with a narcissist or leaving one, these tools will help you see how you can navigate and survive a narcissist's rage. Part of knowing how to maneuver your way out of a relationship with a narcissist is learning how they manipulate you. One way is to triangulate relationships.

TRIANGULATION

This is a form of manipulation in which a narcissist will bring a third person into the relationship and use them as a decoy to subversively control the interpersonal situation for their own benefit. For example, the narcissist might try to make their spouse feel jealous by giving their child a gift their spouse asked for. This tactic is used to pit the two family members against one another and cause them to compete for the narcissist's attention or love. The two people become conditioned to seek out the narcissist's love while disliking the other for any perceived attention given from the narcissist. The goal is accomplished if the triangulation has evolved into the narcissist receiving attention from both people. This is through the unfolding of endless fighting for the narcissist's love and the eventual destruction of the other's relationship. The two people being manipulated may or may not know what the narcissist is doing. Most of the time, they are unaware of the manipulation because the narcissist is controlling the relationship dynamics of the two people from behind a curtain.

James, Brook, and Candy

An example of triangulation is a narcissist who used his wife to punish his lover whom he had hidden for many years. James promised his lover, Candy, a life in matrimony after he divorced his wife, Brook. James knew he would not leave his wife. He was happy using Candy for sex and going home to his wife who knew nothing about his affair. James often subdued Candy's anxiety over the mounting uncertainty of his promise to leave his wife by giving her expensive jewelry, trips, and a car for her and her kids. As far as Brook was concerned, she and James were happy and thriving in a heathy 15-year marriage. James never gave Brook any indication he could not be trusted. He seemed to be proud of the marriage, talked about Brook in an adoring way, and liked posting pictures of him and Brook on social media. James was using social media as a tool to triangulate his situation with Candy and his wife. By posting pictures of his wife, James was making his lover jealous, and reinforcing her insecurity that he may not leave his wife to be with her. At the same time, he was maintaining status quo in his wife's mind. She continued to think James was a good man who was happily married. James used the situation of both women to serve an agenda of maintaining two separate lives. He was happy at home and comfortable with the circumstances if his wife did not know about his affair and if his lover was kept yearning for his attention. James continued to live separate lives, partially because he could triangulate the relationships in a way which kept Candy broken down, and doubting herself by comparing her to his wife but, hopeful. Massaging Candy's hope for a future with him, yet instilling doubt she may be discarded out of love for his wife kept James in control of the relationships by using emotional manipulation and triangulation. Using someone to evoke feelings, fears, or emotions in another person in pursuit of an agenda is immoral.

DISTRACTIONS

Narcissists are good at diverting attention away from them while at the same time, being the center of attention and perceived as a savior or good guy. For example, a parent who is trying to alienate a child from the other parent will create his own landscape or scenario which may confuse or dilute reality. This may or may not sever the child's relationship with their parent, but in most cases it does. Once the narcissist parent has captured the child and formed a strong alliance, distractions are used to maintain a stronghold on the child. Money, trips, material items, and promises are used to keep the child's attachment to the narcissist parent. The goal is to keep the child's attention focused on the narcissist's actions and eagerly waiting for the next show, gift, diluted act of generosity, and surprises to come. This method used by the narcissist parent serves two purposes: 1) creates a perception of generosity and love, thus distracting others and the child from his real intentions to alienate the child from the other parent; 2) heightens the child's sense of happiness with surprises and fostering anticipation for what may lie ahead.

GUILT AND SHAME

Two of the most crippling methods of control are guilt and shame. They have two different meanings but serve the same purpose for the narcissist – control. This occurs over time in which the narcissist slowly gains trust by making others feel safe, unconditionally accepted, sincere, and interested in their wellbeing. This creates a bond in which self-disclosure occurs and trust is established. The victim then bonds with the narcissist in a way which allows the narcissist to control by supplying masked empathy rooted in a fake display of unconditional regard. Your secrets, vulnerabilities, and love are never safe with a narcissist. Emotional exposure is a narcissist's landscape to use and abuse you by distorting reality, circumvent blame when they have done something wrong, and make you feel shameful or sorry for them when they should be apologizing to you. Realize "Narcissists cannot feel empathy and will do nothing which does not further their self-interest," (Jamieson, 2021, pg. 117).

COLLECTING PEOPLE

When I use the term, "Collecting people," the general reaction is a look of confusion – because it is confusing. This is one of the most obvious things a narcissist does to feel and look important. Think of this as a group which is loyal, loving, and idolizes a leader – a harem. The group of people are often mesmerized by the narcissist. What they do not know is they are being controlled by the narcissist. Each person is individually chosen to serve the narcissist's needs. There is a strong commitment to the narcissist because there are usually strings attached. They unknowingly protect and serve the narcissist's ego. The narcissist has a built-in backup person or plan to serve as an emotional blanket to secure their fear of abandonment. If someone leaves the group of followers, there are still many who are available to be lead. This is rarely seen from the inside of the harem. Each person is made to feel important and secure. It is easy for the narcissist to gain adoration and control by exaggerating successes and lying about their life and trauma to gain empathy, and idolatry.

CHAPTER 3

WHY COLLECT PEOPLE?

Why would anyone collect people? As stated above, narcissists do so because they fear abandonment! They do not need to emotionally bond with others, but desperately need people around to affirm the image they have of themselves. They do this by consuming people. Without people near, the narcissist is lost and alone. "Narcissists do not have friends for friends' sake, but they do need people like the rest of us need oxygen," (Jameson, 2021, pg., 25). They also have a fear of being alone. The fear is deeply rooted in abandonment issues from childhood. As a result, they form alliances with others to secure the bond and protect them from anyone who may challenge their perception of themselves. To watch this process unfold is like watching a magician. People slowly filter into a group – it is very much a cult like organization in which those who belong are completely within the narcissists reach and they fully support the narcissist.

LOVE BOMBING

Love bombing is one way in which the narcissist collects people. For instance, it can be exciting and even exhilarating when you first enter a relationship which feels good. There is a desire to spend more time with the person and learn more about their life. This can be fun in the beginning as trust is being developed through a natural process of self-disclosure. This is how trust is built and bonds are made over the course of conversations and sharing time. The narcissist does not wait for trust to seed. They employ distractions by creating a false reality which seem too good to be true. Demonstrating acts of affection through words, material items, adoration, and making you feel as if you are the only person in the world, are ways the narcissist uses your emotions to control you. Examples are delivering three dozen roses to your place of employment after having coffee on a first date. Blowing up your phone throughout the day to tell you, "Have a good day," "I am thinking of you," or "You are the only one I want to spend time with." These things may be nice to hear, but you should consider the context for which they are said and done. On a higher level, they may gift large amounts of money to organizations, loan large amounts of money to you if you are in financial ruin or give you a job in which you have no qualifications or experience.

Inappropriate Gestures

Examples of inappropriate gestures are much easier to detect because the acts are overwhelmingly obvious. Purchasing cars, houses, or providing jobs and attaching an unearned title to their name. These behaviors are inappropriate in part because the relationship has not reached a degree of connection to merit such actions. Beware if you come home from work and there is a new car in your garage with a red bow tied around it. This may sound exciting, but let the adrenaline wear off before you lose sight of reality. This is a warning sign which should indicate the relationship is not off to a good start.

Situational Motivation

Love bombing may be situational in that the Narcissist is in-between relationships and trying to avoid being alone. Narcissists seek relationships because they need or want something. You may be a part of a long-term strategy because you have something they want. Their strategy is consistent in that the narcissist finds what is important to you and focuses on making your dreams come true. This is a form of emotional manipulation used to control you and crafted early in the relationship. They expect something from you in return, as they use their acts of kindness as leverage to get their own needs met. In the end, they have used you to get something they want.

FORGIVENESS

Forgiveness is the most powerful way to regain your power and maintain it. You will learn you are the person who oversees your happiness and freedom from the toxic person. I had a close friend who was married to a con artist. We all knew it, but she could not see this fact. He was basically a walking fraud who was like Leonardo DiCaprio in "Catch Me If You Can." He was a pathological liar who would do anything for admiration, attention, affirmation, and adoration. He let no one come between him and his sick need for fame, fortune, and idolatry from others. He used anything and anyone to gain power and control those whom he could benefit from – until my friend forgave herself for her own mistakes in the marriage. She realized for years he had been using her mistakes in the marriage as ammunition to berate her and make her feel guilt and shame. He was successful at this, as she felt unworthy of love and isolated herself from family members and friends. She had been his personal whipping post for many of their married years. Turned out he was a serial cheater. He even had a second life with another woman and her children. He was doing everything he accused her of doing throughout their marriage. Although my friend was hurt and in shock, she remembered the freedom she felt when she forgave herself. She did not want to live inside her feelings of hate and anger for her husband, and he was not worth the time. She forgave him even after listening to his extravagant lies about his cheating behavior and attempts to make her feel crazy. Shortly after this, she filed for divorce and moved to another state when the divorce was finalized. My friend believes forgiveness offered her the chance to live again, guide her self-confidence, and help her set boundaries within her relationships.

Forgiveness – Self

Forward movement and momentum comes from within. It is available to you if you choose to control the forces within your ability to lean heavily into forgiveness. And because you cannot control others, lean into yourself! Forgiving yourself is something which must occur to successfully navigate life and experience healthy relationships. When others have a difficult time giving forgiveness, the issue is, (much of the time) about them. Forgiving yourself means you "can" be happy. It means redefining your identity. It's discovering you are not your mistakes. It means stop punishing yourself because someone else isn't ready to let you or forgive you. It means see the true friendships you have and abandon or end the ones you thought you had. `

- It means shed your skin and grow — See a new version of yourself.
- It means take back your power or grow the power you never knew you had in the first place.
- It means be free from shame, and free from those who want to use it to control you.
- It means find your voice again. To lose your voice means to lose your power.
- It means stop self-loathing and start rebuilding. This translates to pursuing healthy relationships and leaving the past behind.

Don't be ashamed to move on with your life. You will naturally bring those who belong with you on your journey. Don't worry about those who have chosen to stay behind; we are all responsible for our own happiness. The ability to forgive is unique to us all, and within our power. That said, have hope those sitting at the dinner table with you are working on forgiving themselves as well.

DOMESTIC FINANCIAL ABUSE

Money is one of the most powerful ways a narcissist uses control to dominate a relationship. David Korten, a former Harvard Business School professor states, "Even a little bit of money gives a narcissist a sense of power and domination over others." He goes on to say, "It can begin with the little things like removing your name from the accounts and then grows into stealing, threats, and extortion," (2015, pg.1). When we use the word domestic abuse, we think about various forms of physical, emotional, and psychological abuse. Unfortunately, financial abuse tends to take a backseat to other forms of abuse because it is not as visible, and it is rarely thought of because it is so well hidden.

Roger and Gena

Roger and Gena met on a cruise. Gena was with her family and Roger was with a group. They met while at a cocktail party and were very much interested in one another. They married two years later, and Gena moved across the United States to be with Roger. It was not long before Gena realized Roger was obsessed with money and unwilling to pay for anything. She was a retired assistant to an executive and had acquired very little retirement. Roger insisted she use her money for their household expenses and date nights. He reminded her again and again, that he provided a home, health insurance, and a car for her. Gena was confused because Roger was kind, loving, and very generous with his money when they were dating. It was not long before Gena was out of money and reliant upon Roger for everything. This was a nightmare, as she was forced into a submissive role in their marriage and made to feel guilty if she did not do the things he wanted. He began giving her a set amount of money each month to pay for their expenses. If she went over budget, he blamed her for not managing the finances properly. The emotional abuse continued in the marriage and money was the tool. Gena finally left Roger when she saw Roger was toxic and sabotaged her well-being by forcing her into financial submission. She is in therapy trying to understand how Roger was able to manipulate her and learn the signs of hidden agendas and covert manipulation.

Financial abuse can be one of the most painful ways to experience control by another person. The emotional dominance experienced by a financial abuser is as traumatizing as other forms of domestic control. This is because the narcissist will use money to entrap their victims, in addition to engaging in other forms of psychological abuse as seen in Gena and Roger's story. Sabotage, verbal abuse, and manipulation are tactics used to lure a person into vulnerable situations which weaken their ability to be or become independent. Another example is the narcissist who says they support their spouse's career, but heads off any chance for the spouse to have long-term stability or economic growth, by interfering with her relationships at work. The narcissist may also be savvy enough to disguise control through passive forms of manipulative influence.

Indications money is being used as a mechanism for control

- Suggest you combine your money (into one bank account).
- Investing money without telling you.
- Refusing to let you know where investments are being made.
- Lying about where money is kept.
- Having hidden bank accounts or assets.
- Spending money on undisclosed people or things.
- Having a separate life in which they are supporting other people.
- Making financial investments not agreed upon.
- Stealing money or things such as jewelry from you.
- Using money as a tool to manipulate you.
- Bribing you to get what they want.
- Forming allegiances by using money to gain power against you.
- Using money as leverage.
- Controlling you with money.
- Collecting people by forming financially based relationships.
- Using money to bargain emotional commitment.
- Using money to create a perception of greatness.
- Using money to gain compliance.
- Using your name and credit to purchase things.
- Destroys your assets and things he knows have significant meaning to you.

- Steals possessions which have sentimental value to you as well as financial.
- Lies about stealing when he gets caught. Even when the proof of theft is in front of him.
- Tries to convince you, you are crazy for questioning his ethic moral.
- Punishing you by withholding money or controlling all assets.
- Taking away what little financial control you may have or share with the narcissist.
- Borrowing money from you and not paying it back.
- Threaten to take you off shared accounts or completely alienate you from money.
- Coerce you into selling or signing over any financial assets in only your name.
- Insist you sign a prenuptial agreement before marriage.
- Pressures you to concede to a power-of-attorney so they can sign legal documents for you without reciprocation.
- Insists investments made after marriage be exchanged into investments they had prior to the marriage.
- Insists financial gifts or inheritances be placed in their name.
- Insists you quit your job and let them be the sole provider. "Why not? We are set for life and do not need your income."
- Guilting you into quitting your job to stay home with your children. Insinuating you are not fulfilling your role as a good parent.
- Interferes with your career by calling your boss, coming up to your work, contacting those whom you have a professional relationship, thus jeopardizing your career and income flow.
- Moving money around into various investments without your knowledge.

- Unwilling to be forthcoming about their financial past or present.
- Gamble with your money and assets to "Grow your net worth."
- Put all credit cards in your name and ask you to trust them with your best interest.
- Transfer their debt into your name without knowing it.
- Forges your name on legal / financial document to take advantage of your good credit.
- Deplete tax-sheltered money such as retirement without your knowledge.
- Falsifies tax records and expect you to sign them as well.
- Shames you for how you spend money while excusing their self-indulgent spending habits.
- Appears to be generous with money but, uses it as a weapon.
- Holds people financially hostage after convincing them it is safe to invest with him.
- Cancels their life insurance, changes their Estate plan, or takes your name off other "End of Life" legal documents.
- Spends money on you to enhance their perception and ego.
- Destroy your working environment. They will interrupt your day with texts, phone calls, messages wanting to know why you left the office early.

If domestic financial abuse is something you have not considered or been made privy to, I encourage you to research the subject as it pertains to a narcissist's means to control people close to them. It is debilitating to experience and cages those who become victims. If you are married to or committed to a financial narcissist who is using financial control to abuse you, reach out to a professional who can help you navigate your decisions. Do not think you can reason with the financial abuser or reform them through genuine efforts to save the relationship. Furthermore, take actions which will help restructure the direction of your mental and emotional landscape. You can also take classes to learn how to manage money and balance your lifestyle. As you become more independent and self-confident, you will discover you can support yourself, set boundaries with toxic people, and not be interested in a financial dictatorship.

NARCISSSTS AND CO-DEPENDENCY

People who marry narcissists are oftentimes clueless of their spouse's disorder prior to marriage. They will make statement such as, "He wasn't like this before we got married," "He was never abusive and very attentive to my needs," or "He loved to spend time together and listened when I talked." These are comments made by female patients of mine who are, or were in therapy due to relationship issues with a narcissist partner. These people enter therapy broken, exhausted, traumatized, confused, or in shock. Regardless of the type of narcissist they are married to, these people are desperate to restore their sanity, fix their marriages, find the strength to leave, or change something about themselves to make their spouse happy. In most cases, they come to therapy to determine what they can do to cope with the narcissist spouse and determine if leaving is the right thing to do. Most of the time, these people do not leave their marriages because they have been brainwashed to think they are not good enough, smart enough, strong enough, attractive enough, or capable of supporting themselves. These are all things narcissists' use to control and entrap you. The trick is to create all forms of dependency and massage feelings of helplessness.

They are often conditioned to feel poorly about themselves and robbed of any self-confidence which could change their situation for the better. To make this point clear, you are coerced into a state of emotional submission, at which point you become a hostage to the narcissist. They convince you that you cannot make it without them while at the same time, tell you how much they love you and promises to change. This form of manipulation can persist throughout the life of the marriage and eventually becomes the foundation. This is called *co-dependency,* in which excessive emotional or psychological dependency becomes the catalyst for maintaining a toxic or abusive relationship. Both people stay in a bad relationship because of validating or affirming the other partner's actions by enabling toxic behavior. When this becomes repetitive, the relationship becomes dependent upon dysfunction to function. An important factor inherent in sharing a co-dependent relationship with a narcissist is that the enabler does not necessarily know they are enabling the narcissist.

For instance, when a person is under the influence of a skilled narcissist, they are virtually removed from reality. This is by design because the person is less likely to question the narcissist's actions and easier to manipulate. This gives the narcissist the power to create a personal and emotional relationship of their desire. If the victim is unaware they are being emotionally abused because it's well-hidden in subliminal communication, how do they know which of their behaviors are enabling the narcissist? They do not! This is because once the relationship has gone from rational to emotional, the narcissist is able to distort reality through his ability to manipulate the unconsciousness of the other person.

The narcissist will deliberately create an imbalance of power to exploit you and achieve an agenda. For instance, there may be a pattern where you attempt to leave but do not because the narcissist turns on the charisma, promises to change, and convinces you they are remorseful. This is the point at which cognitive dissonance interferes with your decision to leave or stay with the narcissist.

Their apologies seem sincere, and they are nice for a week or two, but you are tired of being made to feel badly about yourself and always the one who is to blame. These feelings are confusing, but in a co-dependent relationship, the cycle continues until someone leaves or radically changes. Many co-dependents do not leave. This is because emotional abuse distorts the abusive reality of the marriage leaving them to feel as if no one would want them if they left the narcissist. Like victims of physical abuse, emotional abuse creates a feeling of entrapment and emotional paralysis.

CAN NARCISSISTS CHANGE?

Narcissists do not think there is anything wrong with them, hence therapy is for the person(s) who have issues with them. Long story short, the narcissist cannot change. There has been significant research on narcissism and treatment. The overwhelming data suggests narcissists cannot be treated because they have an embedded sense of superiority and lack empathy. Discussions on the likelihood of successfully treating narcissists is a controversial topic in the field of mental health which has led to powerful opinions. It is my position narcissists do not make changes to facilitate reconciliation, nor do they evolve by collaborative means of communication. They are unable to disassociate with the control and power which protect their egos from potential rejection, judgment, and being outwardly vulnerable. Because one of their biggest fears is abandonment, they use control, intimidation, and manipulation to keep others from leaving them. It sounds crazy because it is. They recreate the same fears in others which exist within themselves to incite dependency, low self-esteem, and feelings of despair if left. Ultimately, they create a hostage situation in which their partner feels inadequate and defenseless without them. If they can successfully get their victim to "adapt" to their control and abusive behaviors, they stay with the narcissist by default. This means the victim makes concessions and learns to conform to the narcissist's abuse and happens as their capacity to experience authentic intimacy has been hijacked by their retarded emotional development. They are incapable of communicating their true feelings and emotions because it feels like weakness. Their ways of thinking and identifying with life is so deeply intertwined in their childhood wounds the only way to live with a narcissist is to learn how to navigate their personality disorder. I am not advocating staying in an abusive relationship or promoting co-dependency. It would be emotionally unfulfilling, self-destructive, and toxic. I am saying if you choose to stay in a relationship with a narcissist, you better know how to successfully walk on eggshells. Ideally, you should seek help, and determine what appropriate boundaries look like for your situation. However, this is easier said than done in most cases. As previously stated, a narcissist does not change their colors. They do not have empathy, take responsibility for their mistakes, objectively self-reflect, or forgive. Furthermore, as far as they are concerned, the narcissist does not need a professional to help them change or reconcile conflict. There is nothing wrong with them; their problems are caused by others. They just happen to be caught in the middle of someone else's problem in which they are the victim.

Unlike the narcissist, it is possible to help people who can depersonalize their ego strength in order to facilitate emotional resolution. Most people are capable of this and have the tools to reflect, admit fault, and have grace for others. Do not expect your narcissist to suddenly abandon their ego strength and depersonalize control to reach a higher level of thinking and being. Without surrendering these things, therapy will not help facilitate change or create a path for therapeutic intervention to occur. If you are being abused, find help immediately and get away from the narcissist.

Dr. Courtney Linsenmeyer - O'Brien, Ph.D, MHR, PLC

THE DRUG DEALER IN DISGUISE

Drug dealers have the unique ability to manipulate those who are vulnerable. They are experts at capitalizing on situations/opportunities and are astute at recognizing vulnerability in others. In most cases, the dealer is in a position of power hence, he can use people for his personal agenda. Sound familiar? This is how the narcissist operates, uniquely within the roles he plays. Not all narcissists have the same ability to "Close a deal" because not all drugs are the same or have the same effect on people. Additionally, people come with their own set of needs, boundaries, and expectations based upon their psychological wellness. Regardless of the person, we all make choices, (self-destructive or positive) based upon a degree of self-awareness which is healthy, negative, or a work in progress. That said, not everyone is looking for the same high because we are moving towards or away from self-awareness at different speeds using different vehicles. For example, the rate at which one person comes to closure with the past or forgives themselves is different for everyone. One person may carry anger, fear, and resentment around for life and as a result, be filled with hate, entitlement, and even unconscious feelings of self-hate; it is hard to have genuine fulfilling relationships without past resolution. Without going into detail, the above person is probably emotionally unavailable and likely to engage in some form of self-medicating or self-abuse. Examples are eating disorders, alcoholism, cutting, prescription drugs, nicotine, and being with or around intoxicating people. These behaviors serve to distract one from dealing with conscious or unconscious pain. Although this may be a temporary escape from problems, the cycle of shame and guilt, perpetuate self-abuse.

I use the above paradigm to align with the type of situation/opportunity a narcissist is attracted to for self-serving purposes. People who are easily influenced are targets because they are more likely to fall prey to grooming tactics. Who are these individuals? Let us look below:

> Wounded: If you have had or have relationships with others, you probably have emotional wounds and scars to show for the unexpected twists and turns. Unfavorable experiences, negative emotions, and pain recall from an unforgettable moment, can leave you with emotions which feel irreversible. Such experiences can create psychological issues which make a person feel helpless, desperate, alone, and fearful of the future. Insomnia, social anxiety, and depression are also symptomatic of experiencing trauma. Perhaps the most disturbing reality of trauma is how it can make a person question their own reality. The anxiety can become overwhelming and all-encompassing if panic ensues and feels unmanageable. If this occurs, the person's reality is filtered thru thoughts and feelings which can be distorted and elevate the pain of the trauma. Intrusive thoughts, obsessive thinking and behaving, nightmares, confusion, and memory loss are other symptoms. These emotional and psychological reactions to wounds left unaddressed from traumatic events, only compound the existing feelings of hopelessness. It is unnerving to image, but a narcissist can, and will use the crippling effects of trauma to control and capture a person or situation. They insert themselves into the life of the person(s) who need help, while posing as the savior who is "rescuing" them from themselves. They appear to have what is needed to fix the circumstances and eventually control the outcome. They may also take manipulation to another level by using brainwashing tactics which emotionally apprehend the person by navigating control through a delusional concept of

trust. The person being manipulated may defend the narcissist and fear others might threaten their relationship. This is hidden abuse and mirrors a condition called, "Stockholm's Syndrome." I will discuss this in further detail within the chapters entitled "Emotional Molestation" and "Trauma Bonding."

Because this situation is so complex and the person being victimized cannot always determine what is happening, it is essential to do your best to help them see the reality of their situation. This is not easy and may feel helpless as an outsider looking in. It is not entirely hopeless, and you can reach them if you are willing to be persistent and unabated by the narcissist. If you are the person being manipulated and are suspicious of what could be an unsafe person, get away before you get invested in the illusion of safety. If your gut is making you question your situation, don't question your gut. Misplaced trust is not worth the risk when dealing with a narcissist.

If you have escaped a narcissist who once controlled your cognition, it is essential to seek out a person or person(s) who can help you find professional help. This may be a family member, friend, support group, or counseling center. A qualified mental health professional will guide you through a series of assessments and identify a treatment plan specific to your individual circumstances and trauma. Furthermore, they will educate you on healthy coping behaviors and give you the skills to facilitate relationship choices which are safe.

Distracted: These people are usually overwhelmed with life, or not at all. They may be juggling caregiving for a loved one, working a high-pressured job, being close with family and friends who rely on them for emotional support, or caring for themselves. On the other hand, this person may be completely relaxed and enjoying a life of leisure on an island in the Bahamas. Either way, a narcissist can find ways to catch both people off guard and take advantage of their immediate distraction with life.

<u>Self-Loather</u>: These individuals are easy to prey upon and easily spotted. They are insecure, emotionally dependent, and lost in their own self-hate. This shows by observing their obsessive behavioral patterns associated with themselves. They are commonly people who self-abuse to escape feelings of unworthiness. They suffer from various forms of past abuse and have since then, developed self-abusive coping behaviors that are habit forming and act as an outlet to self-punish. Examples include, eating disorders, drug abuse, self-harm such as cutting, pulling out hair, obsessive nail biting, and burning skin. If they have not sought out professional help they need to do so to heal from their past. Specifically, the help needed should come from a mental health professional who specializes in PTSD, trauma, obsessive compulsive disorders, and/or body image issues. It may also be helpful to research how an Addiction counselor may help treat the behavior(s). This list of professional expertise is not limited to these specialties. This wounded person is likely to choose a partner who is like the person who victimized them when they were young. This can easily be a narcissist who is drawn to those who suffer from emotional abandonment and abusive pasts. Control is easily established due to their vulnerability and unfamiliarity with relationship stability.

Victims of verbal, emotional, psychological, sexual, and physical abuse: The mental health field knows more about abuse today than we ever have in the past. It embodies all aspects of the human psyche with endless ways to abuse a human being psychologically and emotionally. The effects of abuse are life-long and create a plethora of struggles which impede healthy relationship development. One of which involves choosing the same types of abusers creating a cycle of trauma and imprisonment.

Easily influenced: These individuals are naive in one capacity or another. This is by no fault of their own. Their naivety rests in trust, love, youth, idealism, ignorance, neediness, lack of resources, and mental health issues of their own. These individuals are good people who are seeking guidance, love, friendships, or a mentor who will help them navigate healthy decisions. On the other side of the fence sit the skeptics, cynics, pessimists, realists, and idealists. None of these are particularly interesting to the narcissist because they do not offer a quick and easy way to navigate manipulation. Even the idealist has some degree of conviction that is typically defined through opinions or standards which provide a framework for their identity. What I mean to say is these people at their best are not easy to manipulate. However, the vulnerable or wounded person is. The preferred target is the vulnerable person who is wounded. This person is almost like a "Blank Slate." In the mental health field, a Blank Slate is attributed to the mind before ideas have been imprinted on it by the reactions of the external world of people or objects. In other words, the wounded and vulnerable person is at the mercy of the narcissist's mental and emotion creation.

Opportunists: These are people who can see through the narcissist but have a need to use them for their own purposes. In some cases, I guess you could say these people are narcissists as well. For the most part though, they are smart and cunning at manipulating the narcissist's needs to have them in their lives. An example is a real-life story in which a desperate woman with a great need to present the image of wealth manipulates a powerful and wealthy man into having an affair with her. The man in this case was a successful business owner and gained most of his wealth in real-estate. He was on his third marriage and had two teenage children with a wife who was also a successful professional. They flew in private planes, had several vacation homes, and enough money to last for generations. As his wife became successful in her career, he insulted her often and minimized her accomplishments. He told her that her career, "Got in the way of their travel," and would say, "I don't understand why you want to work when I make enough money for us to live and have passive income." He did not understand why it was important for her to have her own identity and money. After therapy and sharing her story with people who were close to the couple, her eyes were open to what others saw all along. He was threatened by her success because money is security and could help her navigate a life plan if she or her husband chose to leave the marriage.

Additionally, her husband would passively degrade her by rolling his eyes when she talked about her day at the office. He was detached from any conversation she initiated. Clearly, he was not interested in her success, offered no emotional support, or desire to communicate. It was not long before she noticed his lack of interest in sex. She was very sexual and felt intimacy was the primary way in which she felt loved. She became suspicious he was having an affair, yet he never left clues or evidence behind to confirm this. While in the bathroom one evening, she had just got out of the shower and her husband walked in. He quickly looked away from her naked body. This was odd, but she did not make an issue of it. However, as this continued to occur, her instincts told her he was having an affair. However, as time passed and managing the process of indiscretions became more relaxed, the wife discovered he was indeed having an affair. This other woman was an airline stewardess on a private plane who worked the flights he took for business trips. She was married to a fireman who was honest, caring, and a good father. She, being a narcissist herself, was unkind to him and made him feel like a failure to control his self-image. Her real goal was to intercept the ego of this narcissistic man who would succumb to her sexuality and be taken in by her petting and adoration for his success. Long story short, she would provide a narcissist supply of attention and become the manufactured self both she and he wanted in order to gain outward attention from the world. This couple is perfect for one another in that there are no emotional expectations other than to fulfill one another's narcissist needs. The problem is there will be an undertone of resentment for one another. This is due to both feeling entitled to receive attention from the other justifying how each individual's needs are more important than the others. The accumulative narcissist supply needed to sustain the narcissistic ego will wear thin as both narcissists are in bondage to serve the other's self-hate.

Please note ... Narcissists are not exclusively attracted to just one type of person or situation in which they can get their narcissist supply. Because they look for anything and anyone for affirmation, they capitalize on a broad range of people. For the narcissist, anyone can provide the landscape to nurture their ego. The more opportunities the better, so why be picky? Following is a list which may surprise you:

The intellectual: These individuals are seen as a challenge to the narcissist. Those who have knowledge or who have paved their way into a successful life using their knowledge are likely targets. An example would be the person who has many degrees, titles, or academic affiliations. Narcissists are likely to view the person's success as a reflection of themselves and enjoy the attention brought to them. Those who are in the public eye are especially seen as an opportunity because it gives the narcissist a "Face" which is seen by a captured audience.

Wealthy: Because our culture is obsessed with money and views it as a significant status symbol, the narcissist seeks it out wherever it happens to be. It makes no difference how it fits into their life, as money is tied to acceptance, approval, and used for personal gain from all angles. They will use others who have money as an opportunity to meet those who surround the successful person or people. This provides a situation opportunity for the narcissist to ingrain himself into the lives of those who can build him up, provide opportunities to navigate his agenda, and use others as the foundation of his journey to become like them. An example is the narcissist who lies about having a college degree, work experience, and relationships. This is particularly common. They "Name drop" and lie about who they have met to impress others. More common than not, they lie about their past and manifest stories which never happened to inflate their image. Exaggeration is a big part of this and mirroring other's stories to bond thru similarities and develop trust. An example is Mark, who met a group of men at his wife's Black Tie Christmas event. He started talking immediately and told the group of men that he had gone to Harvard on a track scholarship. Impressed by his abilities, they embraced him and carried on conversations which eventually led each man into talking about their own lives and personal experiences. This was all the narcissist needed to know. Once their disclosures where made, he was able to earn their respect and facilitate more discussions involving their personal lives. This is a trick. Trust and affirmation are the two main elements which help navigate a decision to invest in a conversation and further it along. The more trust is developed during self-disclosure, the more likely a person is to be transparent and peel back the layers of their skin. This does not only occur in the therapy room. It occurs whenever and wherever there are people who need to feel good about themselves, affirmed, and heard. Believe it or not, this is anyplace where a person feels special, understood, or is given undivided attention and empathy. Mark was a skilled narcissist at building relationships based on faking the realities within his own life to achieve trust and make others feel good about themselves. Before the night came to an end, he secured business opportunities and was indoctrinated into their business circle. He was a fraud who was successful at scamming others to achieve personal agendas. Faking it was easy from that point forward.

Perfectionist: Being perfect is another cultural ideal that is unrealistic, yet so many of us get sucked into the idea perfection is attainable. It is not! With the constant social restructuring of what perfection means, the idea is only an idea. Regardless, narcissists often choose those who are constantly trying to meet these standards, crave validation, and have issues with self-hate or self-sabotage. This person is a breeding ground for the narcissist because the person craves outward acceptance and secretly dislikes themselves; hence, they are always trying to change, with the hope that being perfect will make them happy. Because perfection is a cultural construct which serves to categorize people and rate their value, many who seek this out are desperate for approval and acceptance. This serves the narcissist well, because they can get their agenda met using validation or torture a person by using emotional manipulation to degrade or accentuate the person's failures to meet their goals. This person may also benefit the narcissist in public because they present well and make the narcissist look good. While the narcissist may treat the person well in public, they may secretly emotionally abuse them when away from anyone who may see. This is to keep them dependent upon their views to determine their value and worth. It also keeps a person desperately striving for perfection while simultaneously hating themselves for not feeling good enough to be loved. The narcissist uses this to hold the person emotionally hostage to their approval.

Social: Narcissists look to anyone who can carry them on their back to people or situations which will nurture their ego or give them access to people they would like to be associated with. Those who are social tend to be likeable and easy to talk to. Because of this, they naturally draw people close. The narcissist will feed off their connections in the case an opportunity may arise. Social ladders are examples of this.

Empathic: Empathy is always a good characteristic to have because it shows that a person can share emotional sensitivity, be available to feel other's pain, and have sympathy for others. Although this person appears to be healthy and maybe even stable, they are vulnerable to mistaking empathy for enabling. They can have great conflict when a narcissist is controlling through circumventing blame onto them as opposed to being accountable for their actions. An indiscretion can easily turn into an excuse in which they become the victim and it is your responsibility and duty to, "Let it go," or "Forgive them" for why they cannot change. This situation may also turn into a co-dependent relationship in which both people feed off the other person's dysfunction. If this is true, you are likely enabling the narcissist to continue acting out. Empathy does not mean there is a free pass to abuse you. Furthermore, it is not an emotion which cohabitates with forgiveness in which abuse is continuously dismissed and endless chances ensue as a result. That said, they like to show off their partner in public, but abuse them behind closed doors. It's a bit of a paradox because they need their partner to lift their image up on the outside but need them to submit to their abuse on the inside of the relationship.

Sensitive: The sensitive person is one who mirrors the empathetic person. It would be difficult to have sensitivity for another person without having empathy. The narcissist will prey upon this characteristic in others and use it to their advantage. Co-dependency is also a likely outcome. You must manage this and be acutely aware of your emotional investment made in the situation.

Stable: This person is one who is sought after because they can easily create a resting place, (both emotionally and financially) for the narcissist to nest. They also offer a vicarious sense of stability and hence, bring the outward appearance of strength and confidence to the narcissist.

Forgiving: Forgiveness has taken on a meaning of its own depending upon the paradigm for which it is used. It is no longer just a religious concept involving spiritual repentance and honoring a higher spiritual leader. Books now refer to forgiveness as a means of freeing oneself from the pain others have caused in their life and letting go of resentments. Similarly, mental health specialists refer to it as a conscious decision to release feelings of resentment or vengeance toward another person who has wronged you, irrespective of if they are deserving of it or not. It is used to teach those who have been hurt to give their pain to the person who is responsible for their struggles. Forgiveness is also used to free yourself from the bondage felt after you have done wrong and caused others grief. Lifting yourself up and learning to move forward with your life without feeling the pain of others judgement, while leaving guilt behind to enable mental wellbeing and moving on with life. I talk about this in greater detail within a chapter dedicated to forgiveness.

However, narcissists can use the concept of forgiveness to nauseum. If you believe in forgiveness and offer this to others, the narcissist will take advantage of your belief system and challenge your commitment to forgiveness. This gives them a "Free Card" every time they mess up without real accountability. They are also able to avoid consequences, circumvent blame, and offer nothing in terms of remorse. Enough said. Narcissists will use the different meanings of forgiveness to avoid the emotional responsibility of others, make people feel guilty for their mistakes, and use the eternal and unconditional sense of forgiveness as a perpetual way to circumvent personal responsibility, and excuse their behaviors.

Respected: Those who are looked upon in a way which reflects integrity, honor, and respect automatically capture the attention of others, because they are often talked about and used as an example for others to follow suit. A few examples may include a retired General who served in the United States Army, the successful business professional who broke a generational cycle of child abuse and poverty, or a philanthropist who dedicates their life to serving others in need. These people are often admired and in a spotlight of their own. Narcissists gravitate towards any opportunity to shine and be associated with people who are on stage. This is ego driven and an expansion of self-importance. They will do their best to forge these relationships by lying about their accomplishments. The narcissist also manufactures experiences similar to the person or persons they want to impress.

Showering them with attention and making the situation all about them is another way they gain their acceptance.

Philanthropic: As mentioned above, philanthropic people are viewed as giving, empathetic, honorable, and typically well respected. However, one redeeming fact all philanthropists possess is wealth. This is a two-for-one for the narcissist. If a relationship is secured with the philanthropist, there is likely to be an outward perception of respect and wealth. Golfing, country club references, good-old-boy cigar socials, and black-tie events are within reach, if not "In the bag."

HOARDING PEOPLE

The narcissist does not like surprises and is always planning to secure their future in one way or another. By this I mean he or she is selective as to who they share their time with. This is based upon specific agendas and who will benefit them in the long run. Because the narcissist feels most at ease being in control, their methods are diverse and fool proof to avoid appearing desperate, or deceptive. The first and easiest way to receive attention and hone loyalty is to convince people they are trustworthy. The evolution of this may begin with a show-stopping story in which the narcissist overcame a tragic past. They ran to school every day to avoid being bullied on the bus, worked full time at the age of eight to support his or her parents, and drove a car they had to start with a screwdriver. Impressing others is a tool used to build trust and form alliances. They obsess over hoarding people to neatly and conveniently use at their discretion to lie and support their position. Some people will even "Take the fall" to protect him and his false image. Their self-made empire is systematically designed to bring a profit to his bank account, and secure decisions in which chosen relationships act to safeguard his position and actions. Simply put, they collect people. There is no real intrinsic value in relationships. People are processes and function as insurance policies. They provide protection against what could become a lost or damaged relationship, help to secure risk in the case of rejection, and come to his defense at the drop of a hat. I like to call this process "stockpiling people" in which the accumulation of people serves to rescue and protect the narcissist from any form of rejection or accountability. The architecture of this is ingenious in that it is almost fool proof if you cannot intuit manipulation. It is magical to watch how those who are unknowingly captivated will sacrifice any rational level of independent thinking. The levels of manipulation and emotional bribery is unimaginable.

It would be remiss of me if I did not explain this process of manipulation by the narcissist. Each person who he chooses to be a part of his life has a specific purpose. I will lay out categories below, but please note, there are many categories of people that are not listed, and they are not mutually exclusive. One person may share more than one classification.

1. Colleagues
2. Employees
3. Service people
4. Family
5. Family of a spouse
6. Friends of a spouse
7. Neighbors
8. Networking groups
9. Board members
10. Nonprofit organizations
11. Corporate affiliations
12. Men and women of equal status

13. Their own children
14. People in need of money
15. Business partners
16. Fillers (those who are on the peripheral who act as extras)

CHAPTER 4

INTIMACY AND SEXUALITY

Narcissists have deep rooted fear of their spouse's need for openness and emotional reciprocity. They place a low value on shared intimacy within any relationship but expect to receive high levels of acceptance and affection. Do not expect the relationship to grow and become rooted in shared vulnerability. Authenticity and emotional intimacy are a one – way journey. They want to feel love and acceptance from their partner, but shut down when they are asked to return the same. There is question as to if they can even feel love at all. Because of this, it is likely they construct their own paradigm of intimacy which serves to validate their illusions and interpretations of intimacy. The following story is a good example of how a narcissist tries to manipulate and convince his wife in therapy he is deeply invested in meeting her emotional needs, when his feelings of inadequacy are bleeding out through narcissistic fantasy.

Jack and Carol's Story

Jack and Carol had been married for 30 years and felt as if their marriage was a success. They attributed it to overcoming struggles and learning to communicate through conflicts. They had 4 grown children and 7 grandchildren. He was a successful banker, and she was an art teacher. They came to my office with the hope of finding guidance on how they might enhance their sexual relationship. Jack led the initial consultation and quickly offered his thoughts and feelings as to what their problems were. He believed Carol's sex drive was declining, and this could be the cause of his ten-year struggle with erectile issues. He appeared to be very honest regarding his feelings of inadequacy in the bedroom and felt as if he had exhausted his efforts to fix his erectile issues and their intimacy problems. Six weeks into their therapy sessions, Jack said, "I have thought about this more and have decided that my erectile issues should not be the focus." "I want to see my wife regain her sexual desires and feel fulfilled intimately." I found it strange and a miracle that Jack had had closure with the chance he may never regain his ability to get an erection. Here was his solution:

Jack suggested Carol have sex with another woman to recharge her sex drive which would please him just knowing she was happy. He began by making it clear that correcting his erectile issues were secondary. I did not believe him, and by the look on Carol's face, my intuition had been confirmed. He felt that by bringing a third party into the bedroom to participate in sex with Carol could help increase her sex drive and bring them closer as a couple. She would regain her sex drive and he would find joy in just knowing she was being sexually satisfied. He assured Carol his main intention was to put her sexual needs before his and that by watching her be sexually satisfied would make him happy for her. Furthermore, because he had taken himself out of the equation by letting go of what once was, (his sexual capabilities), we could trust his altruistic intentions. He thought this might help Carol feel more sexual, less inhibited, and bring that feeling of being "in-love" back to their marriage. When she disagreed and expressed her anger and disgust at his idea, he looked to me hoping I would put him back on the train tracks and restart the engine. When I did not validate his position, he became hostile and insulting. Jack felt he had put a lot of work into providing a solution. In Jack's mind, Carol should have been appreciative of his offer. His comment was, "This is a true act of selflessness." In other words, Carol should have been grateful and shown gratitude. As far as Jack was concerned, he was acting out of love, and this displayed a strong marital commitment. What is more, others were unlikely to go this extreme to make their spouse happy.

When he realized that Carol nor I validated his marital solution to finding intimacy again, he made another proposition involving only the two of them. He still held to his position in that his hopes were to please her and his sexual satisfaction was still no longer a goal in their marriage. The scenario plays out with the couple having dinner in a nice restaurant sitting across from one another. Her chair is close enough to his, so his foot will reach the length of hers under the table. Feeling she will be open to this, he goes on to explain how he will bring her to orgasm with his foot under the table without others around knowing the difference. As you might image, Carol was disappointed again with his suggestion, but agreed to try it one evening on date night. She wore something comfortable, and he set the mood by choosing a dark romantic place to eat. To make a long story short, she did not feel comfortable upon arriving and did not try.

You may wonder why Carol avoided telling Jack she was no longer interested in sex. She loathed the idea of having to provide that kind of satisfaction again to anyone. Prior to therapy, they spent many years fighting about sex and intimacy. She was not getting what she wanted from Jack emotionally or sexually. He was selfish and uninterested in learning what she needed from him. He did not listen to her when she tried to communicate her feelings and demanded that she meet his sexual needs as a man. He would become rageful, verbally aggressive, and belittle her if she did not give him what he wanted. At this point, she knew how to navigate her own emotional safety and just avoided his potential tantrums. We eventually learned walking on eggshells was a form of co-dependence, and aggression was unacceptable. Jack eventually quit therapy because I did not pacify his narcissism or validate the perceptions he had of himself. The couple is still married, but Carol is no longer trapped in the cycle of his self-centered ego.

Narcissists will typically flee any risk of potential vulnerability. This transcends their cognitive capacity to share sexual intimacy on an emotional level. They will enter a marital commitment, and go through the motions of presenting emotion closeness, but will not genuinely invest in shared vulnerability behind closed doors. Without this, the relationship cannot grow, recover from painful mistakes made over time, or experience authentic commitment. There is no motivation because the narcissist is always running away from their partner's expectations. You must remember that fear is the driving force which runs the life of a narcissist. They are children living in the body of an adult, who are too scared to take a risk that may result in compromising their emotional stability. The relationship between distrust and their constant efforts to sabotage others, is the way they channel their fear and attain control of those who have made themselves vulnerable to the narcissist. Living with this can be like a war zone in which you are blindsided over-and-over again after the narcissist repeatedly betrays trust and then misplaces blame onto you who is hurt. This is called "Offensive communication" in which power is established by the offender using offensive attacks as a defensive means to gain control and confuse you by manipulating the context of the conflict. It is being the one to take the lead before the race begins in order to feel the gravity of the course and get a taste for what it will take to out-run his opponent. Put another way, offensive fighting is implementing argumentative force and power as a strategy to "One-up" a person and control the conditions of the confrontation.

Mike and Amber's Story

Mike came to me to address his problems with sexual betrayal in his marriage of 19 years. His marriage was ending if he did not get professional help; his wife was going to leave "For real this time." Mike was a successful financial advisor who traveled, liked to have nice things and women surround him, and was motivated by sex and money. These things were the things which provided Mike with a sense of importance and reminded him of "Where he came from." He talked of how his childhood was difficult in that his father was absent, and his mother was abusive. Furthermore, his family was poor, and his mother worked two jobs to barely keep them above poverty level. She eventually died of cancer, leaving him at the age of 16 with a brother and sister whom he was to assume the role of a provider. Naturally, Mike's circumstances were difficult, fraught with childhood trauma, and came with long-lasting emotional wounds that should have been addressed in therapy, sooner than later. However, they were not. As his therapy sessions continued, he was adamant on convincing me his betrayals were justified due to trauma in his childhood and because his wife would not fulfill his sexual needs. He did not have remorse and was angry because his wife, "Did not understand." His life story began to take twists and turns, sometimes adding to the story and/or sensationalizing it to make it more unique. For example, he forgot to mention his mother was institutionalized for a mental illness because she was, in his words, "Crazy." This soon grew into her getting shock treatment therapy twice while in a mental health facility with Mike working

4 jobs while on an athletic scholarship at a college in another state to support his family as a teenager. However, the odds of helping Mike were slim to none, and continued to be hopeless. He had early on in his sessions admitted he had come to therapy because his wife had moved out of their home with their children and was now living with her mother. This resulted in humiliation and interfered with his perception of a good leader at work and in the community.

Narcissists are good at getting attention in what seems to be impossible stories and situations in which they have prevailed survived and overcome.

JUSTIFYING INFIDELITY

The narcissist will often look for reasons to justify their betrayal as opposed to taking accountability for the infidelity. Upon getting caught, they often lie, bully, and circumvent blame to make their partner feel as if the betrayal was justified. This is simply an attempt to gain emotional control over the partner who has been hurt and to avoid accountability. They may even manufacture conversations which never happened to trick and convince their partner the infidelity was inevitable due to a need which wasn't being met on their account. What's worse, the person being blamed may begin to believe the constructed lies resulting in questioning their mental recall. In closing, Narcissists are particularly skilled at doing this, as they understand the deepest forms of emotional control and psychological manipulation. It is healthy to seek an understanding as to why the betrayal occurred and where mistakes were made. It is not normal to be emotionally accosted and blamed for a partner's decision to cheat.

Tori and Michael

Tori was a college athlete on a basketball scholarship. A guy in one of her science labs fancied her and asked her to coffee one day after their class. She thought he was nice and seemed harmless. They talked and had a good time. He was very comfortable leading the conversation and seemed transparent about his life—maybe too open on the first date. He started coming to her basketball games and staying afterwards to show her he was supporting her and the team. He began showing up at her practices and surprising her with flowers on the weekends. She thought the attention was a bit much, but he was polite, fun, and charming. It was not long before he would show up unannounced to, "Make sure she was not doing anything she should not be doing." He would say things like this in a sarcastic way, playing it off as being funny. A few months into their relationship, he began to talk about marriage, children, and traveling together. Tori soon cut things off with him because she had a good chance at getting into medical school and wanted to continue playing basketball. One month passed and he apologized for taking things too fast and wanted her to give him another chance. She agreed under the condition he would respect these boundaries. Their relationship seemed to be going well because he was giving her more time to herself. She was able to fulfill her athletic and academic responsibilities as a student, and she was accepted into medical school. The space he had given her over the past months made her want to be with him when she was available. They even took a three-day vacation on occasion. However, the more demanding medical school became, the more uncomfortable he was with her pursuits. He said, "I am going to transfer schools because I am not important enough to you." She felt love for him but did not want to abandon her medical goals to make him feel loved. This caused arguments and comments such as, "You don't love me enough." She noticed he would tell her she said things in conversations she did not say. He would say things like, "Don't you remember what you said the last time we talked about transferring together?" "We agreed you would think about the benefits of leaving and having a family." When she refused to agree she said these things, he became belligerent. He would punish her by going days without speaking to her and not tell her where he would go on the weekends. When she wanted to be with her friends, he would make up lies which would cause her to feel suspicious of those around her. He caused her to question her decisions.

He manipulated her into feeling as if she needed his approval. This changed her personality. She dressed differently, did not meet her study groups after classes, did not talk to her family as much, and lost confidence in herself. She was no longer Tori. Instead, she was Michael's girlfriend. She eventually left him for her future in medicine.

In 2021, Tori's narcissist abuser died of drug overdose. Tori explained she was shocked to hear this. She thought she would feel relief and wondered why she did not. She understood consciously, she was glad, but did not understand why she did not feel emotional peace. Tori was emotionally abused by Michael for three years and made to think she was nothing without him. Although she was eventually able to get away from him physically, her emotional self was still wounded from the trauma Michael caused. She had not entirely rebuilt her self-esteem and the lingering toxins left from Michael's brainwashing were faintly present. This made Michael's death emotionally confusing. After five years of trauma and grief counseling, she has overcome the anxiety and fear which brought her into counseling. She is making up time lost with her family and friends and spends her free time hiking, traveling, and enjoying her career. She is a pediatrician and in private practice in New Hampshire.

FINDING RELIGION

A narcissist's spirituality is a commitment to themselves first and all other things and people fall behind. In their own image, they are their own and superior archetype. The famous philosopher, Carl Jung defined twelve primary types that represent the range of basic human motivations and each of us tends to have one dominate archetype which dominates our personality. There are 12 different types which characterize our personality and intentions. The list below is a map you can use to determine where you fall and where the narcissist falls to better understand their self-perception of power, and disregard for seeking direction outside of themselves.

- Confession
- Let down their guard
- Sacrifice
- Self-Reflection – introspection
- Being humble – Pride is at his core
- Saying, "I'm sorry"
- Telling the truth – Admitting fault does not have value to him. Instead, he views it as something that could be used against him in the future. Just as he shames others for their past mistakes, he too guards against this very thing. Also, the truth really does hurt. It is supposed to. Pain is always a part of our emotional growth.
- Admitting weakness
- Being authentic
- Being regretful
- Sacrifice

And the BIG ONE, living for something greater than themselves. They are their higher power.

FORGIVENESS

Forgiveness is a powerful thing and is associated with a powerful concept. We tend to attach the word to a spiritual meaning but forget if we do not utilize forgiveness in every sense of the word, we are fostering painful experiences of the past, and living out negative emotions which control our lives. Hate, resentment, shame, and anger will prevent you from experiencing happiness, and keep you from having closure with others and yourself. Furthermore, it can stunt your emotional growth and perpetuate a cycle of the same toxic choices, behaviors, and relationships. The force behind forgiveness is greater than any person's ability to control or manipulate because it is a deliberate decision to close the door on the past, leave the present if necessary, and create a new future. The narcissist would prefer you ruminate in the painful experiences of your past in order to keep you down or disabled. Freedom is threatening to the narcissist who depends upon guilt, shaming, and intimidation to control. This is clearly seen in those who have learned what forgiving oneself means. When someone does this and fully embraces the meaning behind forgiving themselves, the narcissist immediately loses his power. Narcissists do not like this and are threatened by the freedom forgiveness allows from which would otherwise be resolved if we had brought closure.

Narcissists do not use forgiveness as a tool to help facilitate better communication or to allow closure to circumstances that inhibit relationship progress. Instead, they use past conflicts as a form of insurance to "One-up" you in future arguments. Another way of putting it, is they harbor resentment and use it as arsenal to punish. Your mistakes are viewed as weapons to use when the situation/opportunity presents itself. Because there is nothing anyone can do to change the past (apart from forgiving oneself), your mistakes are a nesting place where the narcissist can curl up and settle in.

Because narcissists do not admit or take accountability for behaviors that have hurt others, they cannot reason as to why they should change or ask for forgiveness. You will not get the narcissist in your life to apologize or acknowledge the damage they have done to your life. To not be disappointed, do not expect them to show regret or ask for your forgiveness. Instead, know how to identify false signs of regret. They look something like this: 1) "You know I love you"; 2) "Why would I hurt you? I try my best to take care of you"; 3) "I was not in my right mind at the time"; 4) "I wish we could just fix our relationship."

Recognize there is no authentic regret or apology in any of these words. What's worse, there is a vague message of hope and desire to heal the relationship long-term. This is the narcissist's way of managing the relationship in ways to keep the person(s) close, engaged, and looking at the future with optimism and believe things will get better. This may appear to occur after coming out of a difficult period in the relationship, but it is short lived. It will not be long before the above statements turn into the following:

1. "It is your problem if you don't feel the love that I give you. I love you, but you just can't see it. You should know I love you."
2. "You hurt me all the time and you are never there for me."
3. "I wouldn't have done what I did if you would have .... if you weren't so .... If you didn't make me, feel so .... If you were less .... and more like ...... I wouldn't have to cheat if you were more available to me."

In other words, the pain they have brought into your life is your fault and their actions are justified. Furthermore, you are undeserving of an apology. This is a technique used to overpower those who are victims of their abuse. They evade blame to make others feel as if the abuse is justified or imaginary. As noted in the past chapters, this is a trap and toxic. When we cannot put our finger on the source of a negative feeling, we cannot take measures to avoid the cause or fix it.

4. "If you were more loving and less of a nag, we might be able to have a decent relationship. If you weren't so distrusting and controlling, we could have had a chance. I love you, but your actions prevent us from moving further into a commitment."

Forgiveness doesn't mean accepting the abuse or continue to stay in an abusive relationship. It doesn't mean maintaining a relationship with the person who is toxic. It doesn't mean accepting that the nature of the relationship "is what it is." All these things are what create codependency.

FORGIVE YOURSELF

Because we are not perfect, it will be important for you to do an inventory on your own life and forgive things you have done with or without the narcissist. You can be your prison or your platform. *The narcissist would prefer your pain be your prison.*

Other's transgressions or mistakes are the narcissist's Heaven. It is a place they can go to feel better about themselves, justify doing the things they do and feel superior to others, righteous, all the while tearing the walls down around you.

Because forgiving oneself is so powerful and equips a person with a new unspoken strength, it can be the narcissist's worst nightmare. If you have ever heard the saying, "Fit to be tied," this would describe how the narcissist feels inside when they no longer have control over their victim. If you want to see a narcissist go into a tailspin without a place to land, dedicate and commit your future to a spiritual life greater than yourself. Because the narcissist cannot see past himself, worshiping a Spirit/God is devastating to him or her because of the rejection and abandonment felt by the narcissist through an allegiance formed and honored with a higher power. The narcissist is defenseless. Worshiping a God is counterintuitive to the narcissist's cognition because they are their own God. The only thing separating God from the Narcissist is God does not think He is the narcissist. This is by design. They create their own morality and standards to avoid any form of self-reflection which might contradict their delusional self-construct. What is more, they feel threatened by the thought there could be a spiritual force outside of themselves which has more power than they believe themselves to possess.

THE NARCISSIST AND PARENTAL CONTROL

Narcissistic parenting oftentimes fosters co-dependency between the parent and the child. When we talk about this type of relationship, we think of the mother who guilts her child or children into being with her all the time, or even taking care of her until she passes. An example of this might be making up sicknesses or creating circumstances to ensure a sense of dependency and urgency in becoming his or her caregiver. This is a common theme in female narcissists who, (as they age) fear abandonment and being alone. It is especially true for females who identify with their beauty before other characteristics of long-term value. When their beauty fades, so does their sense of self, and feelings of self-worth. The attention once there is no longer available to fill her narcissist supply. Caring for a loved one who has lost value in life and placed their emotional needs of value onto their child can be emotionally and mentally exhausting. The parent is good at manipulation and often makes the child feel as if they can never satisfy or please them. Unfortunately, this can be a form of control that is constant.

Narcissist parents tend to be permissive or authoritarian in their style of parenting. The two styles are different but, share toxic components of control. The permissive style is characterized as a laissez-faire form of parenting in which the relationship resembles more of a friendship. They set few guidelines, provide little to no structure, and are inconsistent at enforcing boundaries. These parents do not teach their children the skills they need to thrive or become independent. Instead, they create a fantasy world in which the child lives and assumes he is the parent's equal. It is through this parent/child partnership the narcissist gets his unmet childhood needs satisfied, in addition to the control needed to feel safe from rejection or abandonment within a relationship.

Another name for Permissive parenting is called, "Indulgent Parenting." This reflects the parent's high responsiveness and low demandingness. There are little to no established boundaries or developmental expectations. Note, this does not exclude development expectations that can enhance the narcissist's ego or social perception. What's more, this characteristic is not mutually exclusive to either types of parenting; both Authoritarian and Permissive styles of parenting exhibit factors which mirror the narcissist parent's self-serving goal to be "seen" or "noticed" as a result of the child's accomplishments. This parent is like a child him/herself.

You have probably heard the saying, "Living vicariously through another person." Ultimately, this is where the child is treated as an extension of the parent and used to fulfill the unmet or unfulfilled needs that existed within their childhood. Secondly, the parent uses the child as an access point to build his own ego. Success and winning are usually at the forefront of the narcissist's agenda because any achievement made by the child is interpreted as an extension of himself. The intent is not to teach the child how to develop skills by process of elimination through a variety of experiences but instead to choose well and win at all costs. This can be anything from sports, academics, relationships, and beauty. As I have mentioned, the child is used to supply the narcissist with good feelings about himself and acceptance from others. By focusing on the child's vulnerability and desire to please the parent, the narcissist can use both guilt and persistence to trick the child into conforming to someone designed by the parent. This is exactly what the narcissistic parent does to his child.

Another way to look at this is through the lenses of a parent who micromanages their child's choices which would otherwise serve to develop character, strength, self-esteem, and shape the child's identity. For example, a narcissist parent may encourage his son to play a sport the child is not interested in playing. In fact, the narcissist parent is likely to manipulate the child into conceding to his wishes by withholding approval and love. This form of passive aggressive behavior is intended to weave guilt into the psyche of the child – to force him into doing what the parent desires in order to gain acceptance. This is extremely cruel and abusive in the case of a father and son. The father may even instill guilt and disapproval by putting an unspoken boundary between him and his son, one which feels like a punishment. It may also feel like rejection to the son. This is emotional abuse and self-serving for the father. The narcissist father does not genuinely care about his son's athleticism. He is looking at the son's athletic abilities as an outlet to satisfy (compensate for) his own failures. The father may also use the son as a tool to get attention. This is an example of projection.

PROJECTING: A DANGEROUS RELATIONSHIP

Projecting is related to taking unwanted emotions a person doesn't like about themselves and assigning them to another person. It is important to know this if you think you may live with or are close to a narcissist. Narcissists will project their self-hate upon others to disassociate with their own self-loathing. They do this to avoid looking inside of themselves to address their own fears, insecurities, and feelings of inferiority. They aren't telling you "Your" story, they are telling you, their story. Projecting negativity onto someone else immediately shifts blame and makes it appear as if they are not the reason for the conflict. By default, (and in their eyes), you are the cause of the dispute or problem. Common phrases used are: "If you would accept that you are the cause of our problems, we might have a chance." "You are the liar." "You never said that" (knowing that you did), and "You don't have the ability to give me what I need." Try to understand they are not talking about you. They are projecting themselves onto you to subdue their feelings, deflect attention away from themselves, and assign blame to you for their actions.

Narcissism can be outwardly identified. This may be the person who seeks approval through expensive cars, a flashy lifestyle, and other outward appearances. However, there are many narcissists who can only be identified from inside a relationship. They are very skilled at using projection as a tool to manipulate and control others. This can be seen through a tactic known as Gaslighting, in which confusion is created and used to make you question your own reality. Note, this is emotional abuse. This narcissist suffers a fear of abandonment, low self-esteem, and secretly feels disempowered when around others who trigger feelings of inferiority. Controlling people gives the narcissist a sense of security and is likely to instill a false belief that others need the narcissist.

Try to recognize you are listening to the wrong voice! Know the difference between someone who is using you to avoid accountability verses someone who is emotionally stable. If you believe you are, or could be a victim of emotional manipulation, find professional help. Remove yourself from the situation before you start believing you are the person whom the narcissist is projecting onto you—Themselves.

CHAPTER 5

EMOTIONAL INCEST

Emotional Incest is a type of relationship enmeshment in which the narcissist parent looks to their child for the emotional support and companionship which would otherwise be shared between two adults. The child becomes the main channel by which the narcissist parent navigates their self-worth, ego, false love, confidence, and overall need to control. The narcissist's primary source of support, (even above that of their spouse) comes from their child. From a young age, the child is manipulated into nursing the narcissist parent's need(s) before their own. This is akin to sexual incest, in that the parent grooms their child by giving them things and love in exchange for their compliance and allegiance to the parent. Unlike the damage from physical or sexual abuse, emotional incest is difficult to identify. Onlookers do not see how the parent's actions reflect emotional incest because it is right in front of the world to see. Furthermore, the child does not intuit there is anything wrong with the relationship dynamic until much later in life. This is because the nature of emotional incest looks good on the outside, feels happy on the inside, and lives on emotions and outward behaviors we identify as supportive and loving. The abuse of emotional incest is so obscure and hidden, the dysfunction inherent in the parent-child relationship is often overlooked by family members and even mental health professionals.

This is because there is a high degree of communication between the parent and child which appears healthy – and the very things which nurture emotional incest are the things people applaud, looking in from the outside. An example is the father who takes his daughter to dinner once a week for a Daddy/Daughter date-night, in which topics surrounding his marriage to the daughter's mother are woven into the dining experience. Outwardly, his attempts at parent-child bonding are viewed as admirable and idyllic by observers. However, the framework of the father's parent-child relationship is toxic in that he is using his daughter as an object to serve as an emotional agent – to process his private need to be and feel in control of a relationship. It goes without saying the nature of his disclosure is not age-appropriate for his daughter, and confusing, given the content of the message being her mother.

Another framework of emotional enmeshment is the narcissist father who throws money at his daughter's wants and desires which align with his own self-image or is part of his long-term plan to be accepted and admired. An example would be the narcissist father living vicariously through the daughter's achievements as a golfer on the women's US junior league. He would most likely be riding on the coattails of her success, taking credit for being the facilitator of her success. Her job is to practice and perform. Because golf is an elite sport, his daughter will be associating with an elite class of people. This serves to benefit her narcissist father. He will be rubbing elbows with people whom he feels will provide opportunities to elevate him and give him the perception of being important and affirmed. Simply put, the father is using his daughter to channel an agenda to gain an outward perception of success and social acceptance. It does not end here though. Once accepted among the group, his next conquest is to be the best, have the most, and offer acts of kindness to gain loyalty and adoration. An example of this might be taking the entire golf team to dinner every night after a long competition or setting up sleeping arrangements for the team to sleep in his newly purchased RV, made for entertainment purposes and used to facilitate a petting zoo while being the center attraction.

Many parents who alienate a child from another parent live through the alienated child's achievements. Their focus is placed within the child's successes to fulfill their failed attempts to be the success they had hoped to be. Control is the main theme, and the parent strategizes through the child to achieve a goal to win. The attempts to do this are obsessive and become controlling, hence they alienate the child from all other people in their lives, except for those who align themselves with the narcissist parent who is attempting to gain control over the child. This leaves out the parent who does not feel the behavior of the alienating parent is healthy and who wants the child to have a healthy ego and stable emotional development. Therein lies the parent who is perceived as an imposter and a threat to the alienating parent's self-worth and agenda. The following is a true story to help you better understand emotional incest:

Tim is a man who never liked himself as a child. He did not excel in school but had a dream of becoming a successful entrepreneur. Tim's father was a good man but was not able to successfully support the family due to struggles with his own health and eventual health issues with his wife. Tim was the oldest of three children and grew to resent his father for not being who Tim felt he should be. Tim soon became self-destructive and was acting out in ways which prevented him from following his dream to get ahead in life. He eventually learned how to lie about his past experiences and inflate the reality of his life. He lied about having a college education telling everyone he graduated on a basketball scholarship, while majoring in Business. No one questioned him because he was so convincing and had gained a small amount of success. His charisma carried him most of the way through his early years in business.

However, he knew he was a fraud and would never revisit the lies about his academic career and success as an athlete unless someone asked. This, however, changed the more successful he became and the more confident he became in his ability to lie. The story became a platform for his struggle to overcome his tragic life as a child and his eventual success. In his eyes, he was the person whom he had created over the years as a fraud. Believing his own lies was easy and the more practiced he became at lying the more believable he sounded. Tim later got married and had children. He had nothing to offer an emotional relationship and learned as he watched his kids' bond with their mother. This was a threat – Tim felt alone and unloved. The only way to feel attached to his children was to find ways to control them. This evolved through activities, school, and sports; areas in Tim's life in which he felt a failure. They were used to drive home Tim's chance to succeed through his children. This was particularly true with his son.

As it became apparent Tim's son was a natural athlete. Tim became obsessed with grooming his son to become the best player, runner, gymnast, and hockey player. His son was a natural and had the tenacity and drive to be exceptional. His performance on the court, ice, and track was strategic and powerful. These things helped facilitate early success and an indescribable energy from those watching him preform. However, as his trophies and ribbons began to line the shelves and dresser in his room, he told his mother he wanted to quit all sports and was fearful to tell his father. The son's decision to step away from all sports caused division, resentment, and anger in both father and son. Although there were overt expressions of disapproval, Tim's covert emotional withdrawal was especially painful to his son. Once Tim learned he could not control his son's choice to play sports, he withdrew all interest in his son leaving him to feel hurt and rejected. What is worse, he shifted his focus and attention onto his daughter. This narcissist father's actions were malicious and aimed to hurt, control, and punish his son for not allowing his father to live vicariously through his athletic achievements.

We might also see his son was preserving his emotional well-being by setting a boundary with his narcissist father. Nonetheless, the son still felt as if he had disappointed his narcissist father and suffered feelings of failure and weakness. This undertone of disapproval went on for years and still affects the boy's choices to participate in athletics or share his future goals outside of athletics. This is due to the pressure and obsession his narcissist father had with sports and success. His words to his father were, "You don't make winning fun dad. Stop putting pressure on me!" He would cry in the kitchen and beg his father to not make him play. The child suffered nightmares, anxiety attacks, and had sleep issues for years. This did not matter to the father. In fact, the narcissist father decided to take the pressure to another level in hopes his son would agree to play sports again. He started a local hockey league around the corner from the son's school. He funded the entire endeavor and promoted it outside of the son's school. This was meant to humiliate the son into playing hockey through the pressure of other's asking him why he was not a hockey player if his dad was building a hockey program. His father's posturing finally ended when his son told him he was selfish. He also said to his father, "You never made sports fun and I knew you were manipulating me into feeling obligated to play a sport." His father was a dangerously controlling parent but knew how to make his efforts seem authentic to onlookers. The Covert narcissist parent is emotionally sophisticated enough to subvert the possibility of anything other than good intentions and healthy child-rearing motivations being the foundation of their parenting intentions. The effects of emotional incest are all encompassing.

It happens when a parent, crosses emotional boundaries with their child in which the child assumes, (or is assigned) an adult role. Examples range from, the parent's best-friend, "Special person", confidant, or to the highest form of emotional incest being a surrogate spouse to the narcissist. Regardless of the role, the child becomes conditioned to the role of an adult or "equal" to satisfy emotional needs within the parent. This takes on an organic form of its own and is contingent upon the unforeseen dynamics in the adult parent. Meaning, is the child's identity morphing into an adult because the parent is pathologically controlling, grieving the loss of an intimate relationship, suffering from social anxiety, or sees his value through his children's accomplishments and success? There is a plethora of preemptive possibilities as to how parental incest or "Covert Incest" begins. The underpinnings of emotional incest often go unrecognized because everything looks so happy from the outside. The child does not catch on until later in life because parental trust early on is generally high, or because the child does not have the emotional sophistication to read between the lines. This is reckless and according to research, qualifies as psychological abuse.

The narcissist parent is susceptible to engaging in an emotionally incestuous relationship with their child because the parent is naturally drawn to those who will adore and affirm their self-worth. A child can easily satisfy these things within the parent because the child has no real reference point to judge, and they are at the mercy of the parent's presence. This is perfect for the narcissist parent, as the child is a "Blank Slate" of sorts who can be groomed to become the source of the narcissist's supply. What is more, the child is solely reliant on the parent to shape their emotional expectation and regulation, provide approval and guidance, and experience what it is like to be loved and shown love. Children are at the mercy of the stability and mental acuity of the parent. What this means for the child of a narcissist parent to achieve emotional security is a crap shoot contingent upon levels of performance, compliance, and how well the child successfully navigates the needs of the narcissist parent. This too means the narcissist parent has control over the child at a very young age, as children are not often exposed to one-on-one adult relationships outside of family. The child is reliant on the parent(s) to outline healthy boundaries between child/parent and lead by example. This is a springboard for setting standards and having healthy emotional expectations later in life. We learn.

This means the child is trapped until they become of legal age to leave home. Other important factors worth mentioning are narcissists are drawn to and seek out those who are the least likely to abandon them and those who are easily manipulated. What's more, the narcissist parent craves control, fears vulnerability, and can easily manipulate their child, directly or indirectly. This is a tactic they use by undermining or destabilizing the child – by hedging off. The narcissist seeks out those who are weak, vulnerable, unassuming, and ideological. A child is the perfect prototype and can be easily turned into the narcissist's puppet and/or long-term project. Distorting their perception of what a healthy parent/child relationship is they buy their love using material things as an incentive to accomplish a goal or comply to their wishes

It is important to mention the narcissist is also likely to see the child as an extension of themselves. The narcissist parent's self-interest is disastrous and often cultivates extreme anxieties and depression in the child. This is unfortunate because emotional incest is not always seen and can look as if the parent is simply attentive and guiding them into a world of success. The following are things to look for:

High desire to please the parent – Most children want to please their parents; Boys specifically seek approval from their fathers, oftentimes through arduous efforts to win, taking on unrealistic attempts to take on risk, following in the father's footsteps, and standing out among all others. I have heard a father tell his son, "Second place is the first loser." This has become a household mantra which echoes within its walls and keeps the structure standing. This is toxic and can become an even greater deterrent and detriment to the child's healthy development if the narcissist parent withholds love, approval, or acceptance if the child does not perform. This is called conditional love. It can manifest itself throughout the entire parent/child relationship, as it is anchored within the total personality of the parent – how they ultimately feel connected to the child is through the child's accomplishments. This is not a shared love, as the narcissistic parent is using the child's accomplishments to feel good about themselves and as a channel to gain adoration from the outside world. As adult children of narcissist look back and examine their childhoods, more times than not, they can identify the narcissism within their parent(s) and use it as a benchmark to better understand why they have trouble with commitment, fear failure, avoid feelings, or self-abuse – healing or changing their own behaviors and relationships which are toxic to their well-being. With work in therapy, they can identify toxic elements within the family to become more aware of their own struggles, and relationship obstacles that prevent stability.

Emotional Incest is also known as "Covert Incest."

CHILDREN BECOMING A SURROGATE SPOUSE TO THE NARCISSIST PARENT

The child gradually falls into the adult role by way of circumstances, and parental assumptions. An example is a father who the child validates the perceived identity of the narcissistic parent while continuing to provide affirmation and adoration. The child is shouldering the emotional weight of adult reality. Stockholm syndrome is a psychological condition which occurs when a victim of abuse identifies and attaches, or bonds, positively with their abuser. This syndrome was originally observed when hostages who were kidnapped not only bonded with their kidnappers, but also fell in love with them. This may seem improbable, but in extreme cases, covert narcissists are able to make the irrational appear and feel rational. In the case of the parent/child relationship, the emotionally abusive parent manipulates the child into thinking he is looking out for the child's best interest and will always be the protector. During this time, the abusive parent grooms the child into a form of emotional submission in which the child does not consider anything or anyone without the parent's approval. The child obeys or agrees with anything the parent wants or suggests. This is isolating the child to convince them the parent is safe and will be the protector. As a result, the parent receives idolatry, unconditional acceptance, and allegiance. Love in this case is a form of unfelt emotional abuse in which the child is controlled by the parent. Abuse often feels like parental approval, acceptance, and as if the parent is always looking out for the child's best interest. Gifts are also used to make the child feel special and attached to the parent.

CHAPTER 6

TRAUMA BONDING

Trauma bonding is a psychological response to repeated cycles of abuse and positive reinforcement. It occurs when an abused person forms an unhealthy bond with the person who abuses them. (This is mainly specific to Emotional Abuse in which the abused person doesn't realize they are being psychologically controlled and manipulated by their abuser).

The person experiencing abuse may develop love and/or sympathy for the abusive person. In this case, they develop an alliance with their abuser and defend them, even to the point of alienating family, friends, and independent thinking. The greatest control occurs when the abuser convinces their victim they are protecting them and acting in their best interest. The abuser knows the point at which they have successfully manipulated the relationship when the abused person feels distrust, unsafe, or emotionally threatened by people who were once trusted and loved in their life. Herein lies the Trauma Bond, where the abuser's power, control, and identity is masked within the "Savior Role." Their victims are usually people who are easily influenced and emotionally vulnerable. Some examples are children, a person recovering from loss, or one who needs money. Capitalizing on other's weaknesses makes it easy for the abuser to emotionally control their victim yet look as if they are rescuing and/or protecting the abused.

Unfortunately, this becomes reinforced by cycles of abuse in which a need for validation, love, and approval is sought after by the abused. If you know of anyone who is struggling because of victimization or loss due to Trauma Bonding, reach out and encourage them to seek help. For future reference, see "Stockholm Syndrome."

Brook's Story

Brook is a 54-year-old female who came into my office to, "Learn what was wrong with her." Her 50-year-old husband of 11 years was not interested in sex. He told her he was stressed all the time and needed to stop working so much. This seemed to be a just cause for not wanting to engage in sex, but they had not had sex in two years. Although I see many couples who have gone years without intimacy in the bedroom, it is not typical nor is it healthy. This is not to say veteran married couples of 50 years and up are doomed or at risk of emotional neglect if they are not sexually active. Sexual activity only becomes an issue if both people have the capabilities to successfully use their anatomy to enjoy one another, but one person abandons their partner. Brook's disdain for her partner's disinterest in her for over three years is concerning because intimacy has been lost or partially suspended. Physical touch was the primary way in which she felt loved. Her boyfriend was no longer interested in sex and when she asked him why he had become disinterested in sex, he told her, "She was no longer attractive, and sexual stimulation was an issue because of this." He also asked she not take it personal because he, "Loves her no matter what." Brook said she had a troubled childhood. She said, "My dad was mean most of my childhood.

He was verbally, emotionally, and physically abusive." He was always drinking. I would try to be nice and helpful when he would come home from work, hoping he would be calm. It never worked." "I knew what was going to happen. He took me into my parent's room and whipped me for 30 minutes on the bed." Despite the abuse Brook endured from her father, she was closest to her father. He would say, "You are my little sweetheart. Don't let anyone tell you, you are not loved." Brook's father died 10 years ago and she cries thinking about him being gone. Brook often feels sympathy for her abusive father and defends him most of the time. She also defends her boyfriend who is emotionally and verbally abusive. Brook has not yet had a healthy relationship in which trauma has not been the primary bond. She is learning what trauma bonding is and beginning to see what it looks like in her life with her boyfriend.

EMOTIONALLY ABANDONING THE MARRIAGE

Emotional incest between a child and narcissist parent precludes other family relationships from thriving and obliterates the marital relationship between spouses. The abandoning parent, (e.g., Narcissist) is the force behind the enmeshment and controls the direction of the family's overall trajectory of unification. Instead of feeling an overall sense of trust and within a stable family unit, there is an underlying feeling of detachment and resentment from those who are left on the sidelines. This affects all people in the family except the person who is the focus of the narcissist's obsession. Because the nature of marriage is between two adults and the partnership is one of unity, the spouse is affected first and senses it is happening before other family members. Small changes begin to occur which are initially overlooked until there is an obvious pattern of detachment. The abandonment is seen and felt as less time is spent with the spouse and a lack of interest in doing things together becomes obvious. It is akin to people who talk about a spouse cheating. The uniqueness is shared between the two people who no longer prioritized and other things seem to become more important to the narcissist. This can get hidden or masked within a parent-child relationship because parenting requires much attention to the child to protect and guide developmental boundaries. That said, the narcissist parent who abandons the marriage can appear as an exceptional parent. We all know abandoning or neglecting a spouse is detrimental to a marriage. However, when the narcissist parent is obsessed with their child and invested in the relationship to serve their own ego needs, their goal to control is more important than the marriage and spouse.

PUNISHING THE SPOUSE

Punishing a spouse by hosting a higher degree of love for the child than the spouse is a common thread woven into the web of a narcissist parent. The narcissist parent will coach the child or children into forming an alliance with them to punish the alienated spouse. The game is egregious and unrelenting to the narcissist as they will do or say anything to convince their children the parent is evil, cannot be trusted, does not love them, or is threatening their stability. Once the narcissist parent has successfully manipulated the child or children into believing the lies, therein lies higher degrees of alienation and hate for the alienated parent. Encouraging hate and disgust for the parent is next. The narcissist parent applauds the child's disrespect and promotes it. An example is the child who will not look the parent in the eye while talking. Rolling eyes, folding arms, and slumping in a chair while being talked to are some examples. This is frustrating and the narcissist feels in control by controlling through the children. One of the most disrespectful actions the narcissist parent may encourage their child to do is call the other parent by their first name. Instead of saying, "Mom" or "Mother" the child will address the parent by their birth name as a sign of disrespect, devaluing the parent's authoritative imposition. This is an attack on the parent with the intention of equalizing the relationship by patronizing and denying the parent/child relationship. That said, there is no accountability for their actions, as they are attempting to equalize the relationship, if not overpower the parent through a sense of entitlement. It is always expected to be encouraged by the narcissist parent needing the child to align with them and nurture their ego. It is important to mention there are circumstances in which referring to a parent by their birth name is not necessarily an act of disrespect. My comments are specific to a context in which a narcissist parent supports their child's disrespect for the other parent to punish and alienate the other parent.

Parent/Child Alienation

Narcissist parents will look to alienate children from a parent when there is a threat of being alone or when the marriage is looking to end. Parent/child alienation is a term used to describe the act of forming a relationship with the child aligned with a disdain and hostility for the other parent. Basically, it is a campaign to turn the child against the other parent and punish the parent by coaching their children to withdraw physically and emotionally. As I have discussed throughout this book, narcissists are childlike in that they need a lot of attention to secure themselves in their own manufactured "Following" or harem. Unfortunately, this can occur within a family where a parent uses a set of strategies to foster a child's rejection of another parent. This is known as parent/child alienation. In the worst cases of parental manipulation, parent/child alienation is akin to kidnapping. The distinguishing characteristic is parent/child alienation is done through an emotional channel of emotional abuse in which the relationship looks and feels like the alienation is justified. A kidnapping is outwardly seen as hostile, violent, and obviously as heinous. There is no question of the action being immoral, dangerous, and wicked. The difference only exists in the outward interpretation of taking a child from their safe environment.

This is particularly dangerous when the narcissist parent mentors their child into following their instruction to hate the other parent. Sadly, parent/child alienation happens often. The best and clearest way of explaining parent/child alienation is when a parent emotionally manipulates, they are attempting to align themselves with a child. The manipulation results in the child rejecting the targeted parent. Anger, hate and other negative emotions direct the child's perception of the targeted parent to create an alliance with the narcissist to an eventual alienation. It is one of the most heinous forms of manipulation a parent could impose on a family and child. Just like other forms of relationship control, the child who is being affected by the parent's control is made to feel as if everything is just fine and the narcissist parent is doing what is in the child's best interest. Fear is often imposed upon the child to make the child feel there is a need to abandon the other parent and cling to the narcissist parent. The alienation can look as if the alienating parent is rescuing the child from a bad situation, hence the alienating parent looks like a hero. Parent/Child alienation takes an enormous amount of effort and time. It is something which is gradual and occurs over time. Just like sexual abuse, the affected child is under their abuser's spell and manipulated into believing that what is happing is okay and is being done in the best interest of the child. As such, the parent/child relationship looks and feels safe to the child and appears to be heroic to those watching on the outside of the relationship. The narcissist has succeeded at creating a delusional relationship with the child in

Working Towards a Brighter Reality

which they feel safe, and the outward illusion of being savior-like or justified in the parent/child alienation.

The abusive parent spends an unusual amount of time with the child and the relationship becomes comfortable and easy. Instead of the narcissist parent modeling as a leader, they placate to the child's specific developmental stage and becomes a friend or confidant. We will explore this later.

To the few who observe with skepticism and feel "Something is just not right," tend to overlook and be dismissive. Trying to apply meaning to the situation is mind consuming and difficult to deconstruct. The relationship is so confusing to others because everything seems to appear normal and even happy. It is easier to view the relationship as loving, and nurturing. Furthermore, if perceptions of the parent/child relationship look good and the child appears to be doing well, the parent gets applause. It boils down to the narcissist parent creating a perception that is deceptive and well-hidden to achieve their agenda to alienate the child while looking like an exceptional parent. This couldn't be true when the spouse of a narcissist divorces the narcissist. Divorcing a narcissist results in the narcissist feeling shame and embarrassment. Rejection and abandonment are other feelings they become consumed with as they must quickly sort through before onlookers have a chance to judge them for who they are. Furthermore, the embarrassment of being left is overwhelming and humiliating, as a significant part of their image has been destroyed. Because they spend most of their life seeking approval and striving for control, there is nothing more humiliating than being cast-off into an abyss while others watch. This is a situation for which you should be prepared to get ahead of parent/child alienation. Narcissists leave a path of destruction going through a divorce and try their hardest to form alliances with anyone who will listen to their side of the story. The easiest people to form alliances with are those people who are the closest in proximity and familiar – children, family, and friends.

If the child tries to have a relationship with the alienated parent, they may be punished by the narcissist. This is usually done by withholding love or caregiving, ignoring the child, acting apathetic towards the child, or alienating the child altogether. Further examples include, staying late at work, prioritizing others over the child, or saying things like, "If you go to your mother's house, I won't have time to take you to get new shoes." "I will lose the money I need to support your sporting endeavors, affecting your chances to get a college scholarship." This is called, "Emotional bribery." Telling the alienated child things like, "You need to be good for court and stay away from your mother because the judge will take you away from me and put you in a foster home." While this may seem unreal and at best, inflated stories, they are not. All comments came from real life experiences while living with a narcissist parent.

WHY WOULD A NARCISSIST PARENT ALIENATE THEIR CHILD FROM THE OTHER PARENT?

1. To hide their own deception and deceit, AKA cheating on the other parent – In the case of divorce, the child is a pawn used to create an image of being a good parent. (There is nothing worse for a narcissist to be uncovered for who they are; a fraud). In keeping with this, the alienating parent grooms the child into becoming who the parent wants the child to be, and compliant to the emotional demands of the parent. They insist on a commitment from the child and reinforce this by measuring the degree to which the child will be faithful to alienating the other parent. The child is a pawn used to facilitate control and create the image of being a hero.

2. The child is used as a form of emotional insurance – The narcissist parent acquires the child to use as their ego reserve to feel good about themselves and bandage their wounded ego from the divorce. Unfortunately, the alienated child is left to fulfill the ego needs of the narcissist parent. This means the child is the main tool through which the narcissist parent feels worthy. Love is felt through the child's ability to provide the assurance the narcissist is important and worthy. This is discussed later in the book.
3. The narcissist parent does it as a form of emotional security – If they can manipulate the child early on in their development to believe they are the "Good parent" and should rely upon them first, a trust is developed in which the child depends upon the narcissist parent before anyone else.
4. To form a bond with the narcissist's parent – The narcissist has limited insight into their behavior and believe they are the superior parent and deserving of loyalty. This is a toxic bond, and the children are the people who suffer.

There are several things a Narcissist parent will do to alienate a child from the other parent:

1. Tell the child the other parent doesn't love them.
2. Promise to give them things such as a car or other material possessions if they come live with them; buy their loyalty.
3. Bifurcate – say things to the child which are incongruent with what the other parent has said. Such as, "I never told your mom that you should be grounded from your phone." While at the same time, the narcissists tells the mother the "Child should be grounded." The alienating parent is simultaneously

manipulating each person's emotions to establish distance and create conflict between one another.
4. Disclose inappropriate details about marital conflicts. (e.g., Oversharing by talking to the child about personal marital issues). This makes the child feel important and eventually makes the child feel equal or superior to the alienated parent.
5. Hoard the child's time and space to manage their relationships and keep them from any relationship which threatens the relationship with the alienating parent. This looks very different than what it is. The parent often looks as if they are building the child's success or if they are engaged with their well-being. It is never about the best interest in the child. It is about the narcissist and their agenda to align themselves with the child.
6. Over exaggerating or lying about the other parent. This results in the child feeling betrayed by the alienated parent and confused about the love the parent has for the child.
7. Making the child feel as if they need to protect the narcissist parent from the parent who is being alienated.
8. Elevating themselves by making the child feel there is a risk involved by having a relationship with the other parent.
9. Leading the child to feel as if the alienated parent is exploiting the child by talking behind their back to their friend's parents.
10. Making the child feel guilty if they have contact with the other parent.
11. Using a divorce as a weapon to blame the alienated parent for breaking up the family unit.
12. Making the child feel like there is something to lose if they reach out to the alienated parent.
13. Making the child feel they are equal to the narcissist parent. By design, this places the child above the alienated parent

giving permission for the child to treat the parent poorly and feel entitled to do and say what they want to the alienated parent. At this point, the parent/child relationship has formed into more of a marriage with the strength and authority that is bonded in emotional abuse by the narcissist parent.
14. Allowing the child to cross boundaries and act out in ways that would not be allowed when in the presence of the alienated parent. Teenagers will naturally explore and push boundaries as they learn how to manage their emotions and hormones. The narcissist parent will disregard actions that are found to be dangerous, such as using drugs or having sex. Instead of working with the other parent to collaborate on discipline, the narcissist parent will either allow the behaviors or leave them unpunished.

All the above are examples of how a narcissist parent uses power to control the direction of their child's relationship with the other parent. Alienation ultimately serves to sever the relationship between a child and parent. Aside from dismantling the relationship, the narcissist parent nurtures hate, disdain, and fear of the alienated parent. The results of this have long-term effects that are vast and complex. Anxiety, depression, and distrust in others are a few emotions associated with parent/child alienation. These actions are sadly considered to be one of the most egregious acts a parent can do to a child's relationship with another parent.

Mirroring a parental figure who is self-absorbed and emotionally immature can stunt a child's emotional development and derail the child from forming their first secure attachment in life.

CHAPTER 7

WHEN YOU REALIZE, YOU ARE MARRIED TO A NARICSSIST

Once it comes to light you are in a relationship with a narcissist, several things occur:

1. Your world around you starts to make more sense. This is both relieving and terrifying. It's sobering because you slowly begin to realize you are not crazy. Experiences, memories, and the emotional pain are brought together and linked to one thing—the narcissist in your life. You begin to learn you are not the person who the narcissist made you to believe. You are capable of thinking for yourself. You also finally believe those around you who told you the truth about the monster in your life were right. You have a very important decision to make: A.) Do you confront them and let them know you have uncovered their power? That depends. Are you emotionally prepared to take on the anger and verbal abuse which will follow? Because, once you let the cat out of the bag, their

immediate feeling is fear. Fear of being abandoned, rejected, and humiliated if you choose to leave them. Although they are good at calculating methods to keep people close, they can lose. Once they discover you know who they really are, it is terrifying to them and they are likely to panic. And, in the moment, there is not enough time for them to strategize a well thought out plan to manipulate your thoughts while their anxiety permeates every cell in their body. Therefore, their reaction will be highly emotional, defensive, and possibly irrational. Narcissists are not always known to be physically abusive, but if it's the only resource of control they have at the time it can occur. That said, the degrees to which a narcissist fears you leaving highly determines their behaviors and responses. B.) Are you prepared to leave the narcissist? If you are not ready because you do not have a plan, do not expose them by confronting them. Because they fear the loss of control and power over you, any time you spend thinking about leaving them after you have disclosed that you know of their character, is time they will spend troubleshooting and strategizing on how to break you more so you will not leave. As difficult as it is, do your best to regulate your feelings and emotions until you have been in therapy with a trauma specialist who has experience counseling victims of abuse.

2. You start to look into the future and see how things will be different without the narcissist in your life. You can think clearer, feel as if you have more oxygen to breathe, and can eventually understand your feelings and fears.
3. You cry, break down, are confused, and maybe even in shock. These emotions are not the result of grief or regret for leaving the narcissist. They are a reaction to finally knowing what has been wrong in your life. It is cathartic and shocking.

4. Your relationships begin to come back to life and people who love you are proud and relieved. Discussions soon occur with these people, and they reaffirm that what occurred during your relationship was abuse. This is reassuring in that you know you were not losing and have not lost your mind. You realize how the abuse controlled you and can clearly see how your relationship with the narcissist was built on their reality – not yours.
5. Your mind becomes your own again. Your self-confidence is resurrected, and your self-esteem is rebirthed.

When you have decided to abandon the narcissist and feel confident doing so, keep your plan between you and the professional relationships you have established while on this journey. If you choose to tell a family member or close friend whom you trust, just remember these people are your biggest cheerleaders, excited you are leaving the narcissist, and cannot wait to see the narcissist in your life suffer as a result of you leaving them. Forgiveness is on their own time. That said, be careful. Their emotions can overcome the situation and need for a quiet and careful exit. Because they love you so much and hate the narcissist, they could accidentally blow your cover by sharing the good news. The last thing you need is a Covert Narcissist hearing you are leaving them and have been planning this without their knowledge. All Hell will break lose. Remember, those who love you have watched you suffer and are relieved you are finally leaving, but they have not lived with the narcissist. Hence, they cannot fully understand the costs/benefits of your actions when around the narcissist and how much your behavior impacts the narcissist's treatment of you. Be careful and smart.

Do you have a safe exit plan? This is very important. Leaving an abusive relationship is very difficult and often unsuccessful after trying many times. This is because the narcissist is skilled at instilling feelings of helplessness, anxiety, and creating dependency upon them. As previously discussed, the narcissist knows how to get away with alienating relationships and isolating people to control the emotions and decisions of people. AKA, brainwashing and mind control. You and your counselor(s) need to discuss this to great length before you leave the narcissist. Your safety must come first. If you feel your life is in danger, talk to your local police department and file the necessary paperwork that will facilitate a safe exit strategy. This may be an emergency protective order or something similar.

DIVORCING A NARCISSIST

Divorce is a form of loss which creates feelings of shock, grief, and emotional confusion. When two people experience these feelings as they go their separate ways, the worst parts of themselves typically surface and an unseen person from within may emerge as a reaction to the fear of change. Thoughts like: "Will I be able to support myself?" "Am I too old to find someone?" "I don't have financial stability." "I'm too broken." What's worse for middle aged people is the dread of learning how to date again in a world of technology and unlimited choices; all of which are intimidating and a "Shot in the dark." The list is long, but people are quick to assess their perceived value by determining what they believe they have to offer someone. These are normal thoughts and part of working through a serious and traumatic life transition. Many of you who are reading this and have experienced divorce, understand these thoughts well. Furthermore, if you are a survivor of divorce and have children who also experienced this life changing event, you understand the devastation on a much higher level. The good thing is, with counseling, hope, self-focus, and healthy distractions, life does get better and the new begins to feel right.

However, if you happen to be divorcing a narcissist, your journey looks quite different. Basically, get ready for all Hell to break loose. Separating from a narcissist is one of the most difficult journeys to travel. The reality of rejection, fear of being alone, and their child-like fragility, is devastating. They will typically seek out another person, (if they do not already have one), to fill the emptiness in their psyche and latch onto in order to avoid being alone. Narcissist's also make it a point to up the ante by using emotional intimidation. Although emotional manipulation is one of their main characteristics, they up the ante to immeasurable degrees of emotional torture. This can be viewed through acts of bullying, verbal abuse aimed at making you question your abilities, threatening to leave you without financial support, and (if you have children), say they will, "Do everything they can within their power to take the kids." The cause for taking the children is to punish you by taking the one thing that matters the most to you. This is traumatizing. People often say this feels like a slow death in the beginning. It has also been expressed as being in the middle of trauma and watching everything around you going in slow motion. This is symptomatic of the shock and disbelief that anyone can be so heartless and detached from their emotions. If the narcissist is successful at capturing your kids, they will do their best to alienate them from you by forming an alliance with them and with those who are close to your kids. Emotional bribery is the term I use when one parent uses money, material items, affection, or opportunities to manipulate someone into staying in a relationship. Narcissists are particularly good at navigating emotional bribery, because it involves playing to a person's vulnerability and knowing how to calculate differing degrees of manipulation to achieve their agenda. Specifically, children are particularly vulnerable and easily influenced by an authority figure. This is especially true if items are used such as, cars, clothes, and the latest electronics. The most alluring elements used to keep kids close is allowing them to do what they want to do, when they want to do it and dismiss accountability where it is needed. This is akin to unidentified boundaries and dismissing consequences. This obviously makes it impossible to successfully apply tools that instill structure and support healthy co-parenting. Applying collaboration to work in the best interest of the children is not of interest to the narcissist. Their focus is alienation and forming an alliance with the children to add to their collection of people while creating a new reality which suits their perceived image. Children typically want to please the parent. This is affirmed by feeling acceptance and approval from the parent. The narcissist parent knows this and will withhold these things until the child proves to the parent that they are worthy of the parent's love. This is called conditional love. The child wants to gain approval and acceptance. The narcissist knows this and will withhold praise or affection if the child does not do what the narcissist expects. This is a form of emotional control that is never really seen but felt. There is always a price to pay for rejecting or abandoning the narcissist.

You can see that the parent/child relationship is not one of love, care, or substance. It is fraught with control, emotional manipulation, and situational approval. There may be an outward display of affection and love, but this is only to gain acceptance from the crowd and one-up others with exaggerated stories about the child or children. There is always a motive to be the center of attention while using situation opportunities to navigate their narcissism. Children are perfect objects to use because there is a sense of ownership the narcissists has for the child. Basically, they can use them as pawns to create the illusion of being the someone they are not – a loving parent. Ultimately, because narcissists do not get their self-worth through internal sources, they use children or people to get praise while taking credit for their achievements.

HEALTHY NARCISSISM

So far, I have not addressed what healthy narcissism looks like. We all have some degree of narcissism in our lives which acts to propel us upward in our efforts to become better people. Healthy narcissism also helps us focus on becoming stronger, more well-rounded, and focused on things and relationships that bring joy to our lives. Similarly, Michael Maccoby, a researcher and writer for The Harvard Business Review states, "If this were not so, we would not be able to survive or assert our needs" (January 2004, pg.3). It is important to say not all people who are self-focused are narcissists or dangerous to your emotional wellbeing. I do believe most people are good. Furthermore, most are looking for a relationship that has the potential to grow through trust, faith, transparency, and forgiveness. That said, it is important to understand the difference between healthy vs unhealthy narcissism to successfully navigate your relationship choices. You will be more likely to recognize the genuine qualities in people and disassociate from those who are interested in using you as a vehicle to channel their agendas.

A person who is focused on achievement, and highly invested in completing a goal can be mistaken for someone who is selfish and unavailable to others. Hence, they may be inaccurately labeled as a selfish narcissist. Sometimes this could not be further from the truth. This person may be putting extra effort into becoming someone who can care for themselves, or a person who is making up for lost time after taking wrong turns in the past. We also should not disregard the individual who just wants to have something meaningful in their life that they can call their own, and say, "I did it!" This could be anything from earning a degree or meeting healthy goals. These situations are different than the person who strives to be seen and idolized for their achievements, or the person who uses their success to control others. An example of this would be the individual who views their identity through social status and uses situation/opportunity to gain power over those around them. Narcissism in general begins with a person's "intent" to succeed, and the reasons which lay behind their motivation to become successful.

Those who are genuinely motivated to grow professionally and personally in their life are inspirational to those who follow in their footsteps. They display to the world there is more to life than a financial spreadsheet and things of this earth which do not bring long-term joy. Instead, they use their success to navigate relationships that have a compounding effect on their productivity and personal growth. The time they spend focusing on their goals can become just as obsessive as the unhealthy narcissist, but the overall cause to complete the goal is centered around achievement vs. external reward. Daniel Goleman (2018), a writer for the Harvard Business Review states, "Plenty of people are motivated by external factors, such as a big salary or the status which comes from having an impressive title or being part of a prestigious company. By contrast those with leadership potential are motivated by a deeply embedded desire to achieve for the sake of achievement." This does not mean there is a financial demarcation by which we define the difference between healthy and unhealthy narcissism. Nor am I implying that highly achievement oriented people are unhealthy if they own nice things. This goes back to the motivation behind winning, meeting financial goals, lifestyles etc. The narcissist is most likely motivated by gaining acceptance and approval. They will live to their limits to be accepted into an upper-class group of people and rub elbows with them on the country club golf course. Healthy narcissism does not look like this. For example, aspiring to play golf can be motivated by filling one's time after retirement, fulfilling a goal which has been put off, or meeting people who have like interests. They do set out to use golf to meet people who will give them access to a lifestyle where the narcissist uses families to gain opportunities to mask success.

A NARCISSIST'S FEAR OF THE THERAPY ROOM

Narcissists do not think it is necessary to seek mental health advice to better understand conflict within themselves or with others. This is because they do not believe there is anything wrong with them. If there is conflict, it is because of something someone else did. They believe they are perfect and do not understand why anyone would think any differently. Nothing is ever their fault and if others have an issue with them, it is their problem, and the narcissist is not liable for conflict. Nonetheless, narcissists do find their way into the therapy room, but not on their own volition or on account of self-awareness. Their relationship with counseling is tied to others who are in their lives and people whom they have cheated. These people are usually at the end of their rope and threatening to leave the narcissist after other attempts to fix things on their own have failed. The relationship is hanging on by a thread and often struggling to unweave a web of co-dependency and abuse. What's more, narcissists will land in a therapist's room because they have been ordered by the court system to be assessed or as a last-ditch effort to stay out of jail. If either of these reasons are the cause, they do what they can to control the therapy sessions and convince the therapist they are not the bad person and others are to blame for their actions. Hence, their efforts are made to debunk the system and prove everyone wrong by a getting a "Pass" from the mental health professional. In other words, they show their best face and work hard to establish a false self; one that is kind, safe, and emotionally sound. They also try their best to create the illusion of being the victim. Everyone just has it, "All wrong."

> *The Narcissist can be the victim, the hero, but never the villain.*
> *Unknown author*

Narcissists react in predicable ways when brought into the therapy room. They can be defensive and dominate the session. The reason for this is two-fold. First, they intimidate the person who is in therapy with them and take advantage of the opportunity to be on stage. They turn the therapy room into a platform where they create their own reality. As previously mentioned, a narcissist likes to be the center of attention, is charming at times, and knows how to manipulate complex situations that involve relationship dynamics. This last characteristic is more aligned with a sociopath, but an intelligent narcissist, (who does not meet all characteristics of a sociopath) can pull this off. As a side note, one of the hardest things for a narcissist to do is *temper* their outward efforts to be the center of attention. Because of this, it is difficult for them navigate the higher degrees of manipulation that a sociopath can master.

If the narcissist does not verbally dominate the therapy session, they do this through acting detached and apathetic. Their body language is overwhelmingly obvious and used to make others in the therapy session feel guilty, insignificant, stupid, or weak. They may be mad because they have been put in a situation that requires their cooperation, honesty, time, and collaboration. The narcissist is only a part of the therapy process because they have something to lose if they are not there. It has been my experience this is overwhelmingly true. Recall that a narcissist does not believe there is anything wrong with them and conflict is always someone else's fault.

Many therapists are not trained to take on a narcissist in their therapy room. This is not something they teach you in school and Narcissism is not a specialty per se.' This is partly because narcissists do not feel there is anything wrong with them, hence they do not seek therapy. Where a person who is depressed or anxious may reach out to get metal health help, the narcissist has no self-awareness. However, on the other side of the narcissist is the train wreck left behind when they are through victimizing someone. Narcissism is addressed by therapists and clinical psychologist who specialize in trauma, abuse, and other areas where victimization occurs. Narcissism finds its way into the therapy room through the pain of others. Not through the narcissist seeking to better themselves.

Lyla and Jayson

Lyla and Jayson were both successful in their own professions. They put off having children and agreed to invest their money early in the marriage so they would have passive income sooner than later. The couple grew in their careers and money seemed easy to make and saving was not an issue. As both people got closer to nearing the end of a decade, they talked more about children and decided to get pregnant. Lyla did not see a reason to quit working and Jayson fully supported her. However, as Lyla became closer to having their child, Jayson became less supportive and spent more time working. He would come home later, travel more, and communicate less. Lyla said, "It almost felt like he was punishing me." When she would ask him to work less and help her get the house ready to have the baby, he was negative and acted resentful. He soon began blaming her for his actions and temper. He was easily angered and was not interested in talking about the baby. It felt as if Jason was jealous that Lyla was beginning to develop a relationship with their unborn baby. This was not Jayson, and Lyla could not understand why he had seemingly changed from wanting to have a life with her and a family. She begged him to go with her to talk with a marriage counselor, but he refused. She did not want to go without him but felt it was better if she went solo if he would not go. One month passed and she had had four sessions with her counselor. She was no closer to understanding Jayson but was learning that Jayson's issues are his own. If he would not make himself available to talk about his feelings, Lyla could not make their marriage work on her own. She told him she was learning and growing in her sessions with the counselor and hoped he would decide to join her before the baby was born. Jayson reminded her that their marital problems rested on her shoulders and if she did not change, they could not have a good marriage. As far as he was concerned, he did not need therapy and any issues in their marriage were caused by Lyla. He would say things like, "You are too sensitive." "I'm sorry you feel that way." "You should just try harder to be a good wife." The emotional detachment continued as did the verbal abuse. Albeit Jayson's abuse, and refusal to attend counseling sessions, Lyla was persistent in her career, counseling and preparing to be a mother of a daughter. After she had the baby, the manipulation and verbal abuse got worse. He did not form an attachment to their daughter and ignored Lyla. The more time Lyla spent with their daughter, the more verbally abusive he was to Lyla and the more negative he was about having a child. Lyla was living in a nightmare and feeling as if she was a single parent, whose legs were being kicked out from under her every time she would stand. After 10 years into the marriage, and 5 years of counseling, Lyla felt as if she was at an impasse. She could not raise her daughter in the emotionally abusive environment with a husband and father who was not emotionally attached to her or the children. Her counselor asked her to do an emotional/cost/benefit/analysis of the pros and cons of leaving vs staying. Lyla divorced Jayson on their 11th year anniversary. She has since remarried to a man who is emotionally available, supportive, and loves her and her daughter unconditionally. Her daughter is 25 and works as a forensic accountant. After years of counseling on her own, she does not speak to her father.

Sally and Dane

Sally met Dane at a mutual friend's birthday party. Dane was very charismatic, dressed well, showed interested in Sally, and seemed very respectful. Throughout the evening, Sally learned he had 3 grown children. His oldest son was a chemist who went to school at MIT, graduating with honors. His middle child was a pediatrician at Johns Hopkins and married with twin girls. His youngest was an engineer for an oil and gas company in Texas and getting married soon. He seemed very well adjusted and was soon retiring from a position as the CEO of a local hospital. This made sense. He was someone who had high expectations of himself and in turn, had high expectation of his children. Sounds good, doesn't it? As the evening continued, Dane talked about his academic endeavors, basketball scholarship, love for hunting, and family experiences of a child of 9. Sally also shared her story and delighted in some of the similarities. She was one of 8 children and laughed about getting overlooked at times because she was always competing for attention from her parents. Both people were having a good time and delighting in each other's company. Dane excused himself for a moment to go to the Men's Room. As Sally sat and reflected on their conversation, she realized that Dane did not mention the mother of his children. Sally found this to be odd. The longer they talked, the more she noticed he appeared to be avoiding discussing his past relationship with his wife. When she asked, "Where did you meet your wife?", he answered and quickly changed the subject. When Sally continued to casually inquire about his wife through normal means, he was short and appeared agitated. At this point, Sally felt as if she had crossed a boundary and did not continue asking questions. As the night when on, they sat together at the bar and began to wind down.

However, a close friend of his who had too much to drink came over to the bar and asked if he was still dating "That girl who broke up his marriage." Furthermore, the friend continued to disclose the details of Dane's marital issues. This was very inappropriate, but the friend was drunk. He told Sally that in college, Dane was a "Player" and could get any girl to do what he wanted them to do. He also told her he had been married three times and cheated on each of his wives. This was disturbing to Sally, but she now knew why Dane was trying to avoid talking about, (what she thought to be) the mother of his children. When Dane returned to the bar, his friend was still there with Sally. Because she had a different perspective of his reality and knew about some of his past, she stopped offering further information about herself and began to ask Dane more pointed questions such as, "When did you decide to have children?", "Does your wife work?", "What made you decide to marry?" Placed in this order, it was impossible for him to divert the conversation to avoid answering the questions. Sally put him in a situation where he would have to answer the questions or act out in anger. He was not going to do this because he liked Sally. He finally disclosed he had been married three times, but never truly loved anyone until he married his third wife. He made it seem magical and as if he worshiped her. Life was great until she "Lost her mind" according to him. Dane told her an elaborate story about how his late wife had issues with depression and addiction. It all began when he started traveling. Dane explained that she became "Needy," and would not stop obsessing about the possibility of him cheating on her while he was away. Dane explained she would intentionally start arguments and do things to herself to get his attention. Eventually, he said that she locked herself in the bathroom and would not come out for days. Now, this in not typical dinner conversation, nor is it appropriate. However, the narcissist can create or exaggerate stories to circumvent any pressure to participate in a social setting that merits mutual reciprocity. Later in the evening when Sally was taking a break from the setting with Dane and his friend, a female approached her and asked if Sally was dating Dane. She said, "No." The female told her he was abusive and always seemed to slide by without accountability.

Women were commodities, and Dane felt entitled in the workplace to make sexist comments and belittle women who were in high positions of leadership. This was disturbing to Sally, and she decided at that point to leave the social event and distance herself from Dane. She later found out that he was emotionally abusive to his wife, and she fled him to find peace and recapture her stability and self-worth. As it pertains to her, "Depression, self-abusive behaviors, and isolating herself in the bathroom, everything was a lie. She did suffer the effects of trauma due to his emotional abuse, but eventually learned coping skills to gain closure with her abuser, Dane. Although it is not known, it is likely that his first and second wife were also labeled as crazy or made to look like monsters by Dane.

James and Brooklyn

Brooklyn met James at a wedding in Belize. Both people knew the couple getting married and were at the wedding alone. Brooklyn was recently divorced, and James was going through a divorce. They exchanged conversations and enjoyed the few days in Belize. One year later, the couple ran into one another at a funeral. The coincidence was bazar and funny at the same time. They took the encounters as a sign to proceed with seeing one another more often.

The relationship took off and was fast and furious. They were both childless and did not have many responsibilities apart from a mortgage payment and house pets. They went to dinner on the weekends, virtually connected when they were apart, and soon became engaged. Two years later, they were married and planning a future. Brooklyn wanted to go back to school and get a master's degree in engineering. James was living on a trust fund and saw no reason for her to get another degree. He saw this as a waste of time and interfering with the future he had envisioned. After enrolling in school, James began to make comments which seemed to be complimentary, but left Brooklyn wondering what James "Really meant." He would say, "I am proud of you, but we could be in Italy right now if you weren't in school." Despite the confusion, Brooklyn ignored James and completed her master's degree in chemical engineering. James seemed supportive but began to sabotage her relationships with family and friends when she was offered a job at a chemical plant. He felt there was no room in her life for him. This became an issue at work as well because he was jealous of her co-workers. She was quick to tell him he needed to get help for his possessiveness and that she would not allow this to continue in the marriage. He immediately said, "No." He believed her decisions had created the problem and his actions were justified. She gave him and ultimatum in that if he did not go get help, she was going to leave. After months of arguing over this, he finally went with her. His aggressiveness was immediately shown in the first session. He yelled at her and would not take accountability for his jealous outrages. He tried to intimidate and provoke the therapist but was unsuccessful. This left James upset and resentful upon leaving the first session. Two weeks later, James showed up alone. Although narcissists do not go to therapy alone, they do when there is something or someone to lose. In this case, Brooklyn was still holding onto her threat of leaving the marriage if he did not get help. He walked into his session apathetic and as if he had had been unjustly sent to his room. Yes, he was acting a child. He tried to make the therapist feel sorry for him and appear to be the real victim. Lies followed and more lies followed. It was as if he was creating his own reality. He was! When the therapist caught on and confronted him on his lies, he became defensive and indignant. At this point, the therapist explained she was not going to placate to his manipulation and that if he wanted to stay in therapy, he would play by her rules. James had been called out on his behavior by someone who he could not manipulate and who could call him out for who he was, a narcissist. He was not willing to proceed with counseling and Brooklyn decided to file for a separation. She moved into a rent house near her work. James became angrier and desperately wanted her to come home. He was willing to change, but Brooklyn knew he could not. He lied about seeing his own therapist and promised her that he had changed. He had not and would not.

It is impossible to help a couple when one is unwilling to take accountability for their actions.

ARE YOU MORE AFRAID OF LEAVING OR STAYING IN AN UNHEALTHY RELATIONSHIP?

Leaving doesn't have to be scary. Unfortunately, fear is what keeps people in toxic relationships. Not knowing what life looks like outside of the relationship can be intimidating. If it's abusive, (emotional, verbal, psychological, or physical), control is probably a factor which will foster feelings of insecurity and make you feel as if you cannot make it on your own. Don't believe this. Your abuser needs you and has probably made you feel as if you need them. Believing that you cannot succeed without them is a trap which will dismantle your self-confidence and cause you to feel you have no other choice. What's worse, the longer you stay, the more you believe this lie and rationalize why you continue to stay with them. Common themes are:

1) "I cannot support myself."
2) "Who is going to want me?"
3) "I cannot leave my kids."
4) "He/She needs me."
5) "It's really not that bad."

Here is the reality: If you do stay in a relationship with your abuser, the relationship becomes more toxic by manifesting itself within codependency. Your fear of leaving feeds their fear of losing you and in turn, incites their desperate attempts to keep you captive through control and abuse. Regardless, the decision to leave or stay is probably determined by weighing the costs and benefits of what's known versus unknown. Staying in the relationship likely seems easier because you are familiar with the dysfunction hence, you can predict oncoming conflict and adjust accordingly. Said another way, you know how to navigate the toxic parts and apply damage control when needed. Leaving on the other hand is unsettling, unpredictable, and starting over is a long journey. It is, but it begins by understanding that your abuser does not love you. They love power and control. Staying feeds this and further affirms that they do not care. Once you leave, they will replace you with another person who will reflect at them what they need to see and feel about themselves. Talk to a professional in the mental health field to help you learn, how and why this person became a part of your life. You need to know this, as you do not want to choose the same person in a different skin.

The ambiguity of the future might feel impossible to process but leaving will allow you access to freedom.

WHY WOULD ANYONE STAY IN AN UNHEALTHY RELATIONSHIP IF THEY KNEW IT WAS UNEALTHY?

This is the biggest question everyone is asking you and themselves. Why do you continue to stay with this person who is so toxic? The following question is, "Can't you see they are never going to change?" and "They are abusive and emotionally dangerous." What's worse is the pitied side to side headshake and look of disbelief as to why you stay. How can you stay in an unhealthy relationship knowing it is painful?

These questions are constantly asked to the victim of a narcissist. So much so they are impervious to the meaning behind the question. If you have never been the victim of abuse, it will be difficult for you to understand. They stay because the narcissist has made them believe they do not have other options, are not good enough, pretty enough, smart enough, or have the resources to make it on their own. As previously discussed, they feel helplessly dependent upon the narcissist and will even defend their narcissist's abusive behavior. Below are common things the victim of a narcissist will say to justify why they stay with their abuser:

1. "They will change. I am going to counseling and he/she promised to find their own counselor."
2. "He/she had a traumatic childhood and I need to be more compassionate."

3. "He/she is just stressed and anxious because they work so much." This is a very common excuse followed by, "He/she is a good parent and just works hard to be a good provider."
4. "He/she has never been loved by anyone other than me. I need to be patient."
5. "He/she always comes back to me, so he/she must love me."
6. "Everyone in his/her life has abandoned them. I cannot leave them like everyone has in the past."
7. "I cannot afford to leave. He/she controls the finances and I have not worked for years."
8. "It is my fault."
9. "I just need to love him more."
10. "Leaving will disrupt the family and the kids will suffer as a result."
11. "I fear being alone." Narcissists are skilled at tearing down your self-esteem and alienating you from your family and friends.

An overarching excuse is the fear of being alone. Although this may not seem like an excuse, it is a commonly said reason as to why people stay with a narcissist. Furthermore, it may be disguised within one of the above reasons. The fear of being alone is usually instilled by the narcissist who needs you to stay with them. Fear is what keeps you close and dependent on them. You may even look back to who you were before you met the narcissist and wonder what happened to that person, as you look in the mirror and see a person who is making excuses to stay with the narcissist who is hurtful. If you have never known freedom from a narcissistic relationship and are reading this book, know you can become your own person. Try to embrace there is security outside of the narcissist relationship. They cannot overpower your will to be free if you just leave and cut off any access for which they may use to re-enter your life. This does not mean cut your children out of your life if this is your tie to the narcissist. Use caution and professional help to navigate family relationships, because a shared relationship had with the narcissist is a bloodline to manipulate you and those which link you to them.

EMOTIONAL ABUSE AND THE IMPACT OF STAYING

So far, I have only touched on the horrifying experiences and effects of living with or around a high functioning narcissist. In the beginning it feels as if they are the most generous, loving, and safe people in which you could find yourself. Their kindness and gentle ways of making everything seem easier and less stressful is alluring and contagious. The effects of this are so overpowering in the moment, being yourself feels safe, and transparency knows no boundaries. Self-disclosure flows freely and seems indescribably right. At this point, you now understand this is only the beginning of a torturous relationship and the narcissist's never-ending pursuit of control.

The abuse begins under the surface where subtle things "Just don't feel right," and get dismissed because the cause is so innocuous. The Covert narcissist's manipulation is so sophisticated you cannot be exact as to why you feel strange or weird. It is not clear until you begin to feel isolated or pressured by the narcissist to be with them all the time, or at their disposal. Because you cannot always be with the narcissist, they will begin to feel insecure about your loyalty and threatened by your life outside of them. This includes your career, personal relationships, family relationships, and any situation which may propel you into new opportunities to succeed. Because they perceive these situations as a threat, the narcissist will begin to isolate you from these relationships. The narcissist will look for reasons as to why a certain friend is a bad influence on you or try to convince you the friend is not a "True friend." Instead of going to dinner with them, you decide to stay home with the narcissist until you are no longer a part of a friendship group your alienated friend belonged to as well. The narcissist has succeeded in alienating you from all your friendships. It goes without saying the impact of this is hurtful, feels lonely, and an emotional trap if you do not leave. The longer you stay with the narcissist, the less control you have over your own life. The narcissist will also attack your family to drive a wedge between you and them. They may make excuses as to why you cannot visit them for the holidays and alienate your children from your family.

Anxiety is an issue which can become overwhelming and may gradually evolve into acquiring a panic disorder. Not feeling safe, questioning your relationships, and feeling alone while not understanding your situation is horrifying. Staying with a narcissist gravely affects your mental health and can make you feel as if you are the problem. Depression, obsessive compulsive disorder, and self-abuse are common mental health issues and symptomatic of living and staying with a narcissist.

Your identity becomes swallowed by the narcissist's need for attention, as they use you as a platform for their own identity. The narcissist sees you only to navigate their ego, leaving you with little time to navigate your own life. When you no longer have your own identity, there is little chance to develop self-confidence or healthy self-esteem. This is because the narcissist is building their own self-worth through you. They also manipulate you into acquiescing in other areas which impact your life long-term.

There is never an effort to work through conflicts in a collaborative way which supports resolution. This is because they believe they are always right and, on a track to prove you are wrong. This becomes a "Beat Down" in which emotional and psychological torture causes you to submit to their reasoning. Even when you both know the narcissist is wrong, the narcissist will never admit it. You will not get an apology because they do not have remorse. This will become exhausting and wear on your confidence and mental health.

Staying with a narcissist comes with many ramifications with lasting and impactful effects on your life. The overriding issue is the degree to which the emotional abuse has on your life. The above explanations have a direct impact on your mental health. Loss, isolation, alienation, verbal abuse, psychological abuse, and emotional control are factors that dismantle your mental stability. This is their agenda, and you must take this into consideration when evaluating the costs and benefits of staying with a narcissist.

PULLING THE TRIGGER

"Leaving a narcissist is like trying to climb out of a fire hole using a metal ladder. The climb is torturous, and you question if escaping is worth the wounds that will ensue as a result. You must remember if it feels wrong, it is wrong, and abuse is never right. Freedom is worth every step."

CHAPTER 8

HOW TO HEAL

It is important to expect the world and people will challenge your life and make you feel like things are hopeless at times. You will experience merciless pain and problems which peak to a place of hopelessness; a place which force thoughts and questions about the meaning of life. These are inevitable experiences which fuel feelings of depression and anxiety. There is no way around this if you are realistic and accept that pain is inevitable in order to grow and thrive. Having closure does not mean you are agreeing, enabling, or turning a blind eye to the problem. You may feel very uncomforted, and as if you are betraying a child or enabling the person who is an abuser; This could not be further from the truth. It means accepting the truth, letting go of anger and hate, and finally forgiving (emotionally abandoning) the person(s) who betrayed you. You decide what this means to you. Forgiveness is understood through how you invest in your spirituality and how you experience a path with your higher power. Hopefully, you have formed a relationship with a higher power. The path to freedom from bondage requires learning, hope, faith, and direction. Understand these things are not inherently embodied within your makeup. We are not born or blessed with the organic skills to emotionally sustain ourselves. Furthermore, only a narcissist believes he is capable of housing such powers. I hope you understand this, and if you do not, do your research.

Be open to taking measures which help facilitate empathy and understanding. This does not mean take back the person who abused you and it does not mean to condone their behavior or sickness. This means learn how to disassociate the effects of your pain from the person who caused it. They are not a part or factor in your healing, therefore leave them behind as you recreate yourself without the narcissist taking up space in your head and new life ahead. Invest in your ability to take control over your life. If you do not do this, the narcissist wins. You must trust in order to create peace, surrender your pain, (or suffer in bondage), and forgive to abandon the person who nearly destroyed your life. You should not attempt to train this process down the railroad alone. Use your head and begin to lead.

There are no quick fixes to unpack your emotions, process the past and release emotions caused by trauma, but it is possible. It can be the hardest thing to imagine for those who are in the middle of crisis with a narcissist. The gravitational pull to stay can be exhausting and encumber your ability to execute necessary steps to leave the narcissist. This is truer for those who are in established relationships and for those who have made long-term emotional investments in the narcissist. Regardless, the journey to escape and become the director of your life is within reach. You must not feed into the narcissist's attempts to hold onto you, and you must try to be transparent with yourself—especially if you feel there is a chance to become free—this is always possible.

FACING YOUR FEAR OF CHANGE: BE HONEST WITH YOURSELF

Although this is a book about Narcissism and learning to how to heal from a narcissist's abuse, it is important to determine if there is anything you are doing or not doing which is preventing you from using what power you may have to leave. It is possible you may be making excuses as to why the narcissist is still in your life. I say this to help you recognize that, if you are making excuses to stay in the relationship, you ultimately have the power to leave. Recognize the narcissist has not entirely taken over your ability to think for yourself. If you could help yourself, what would you do? Establish a career to free yourself from a narcissist? Fix the relationship? Heal your pain caused by the narcissist? Learn how to navigate the narcissist's ego to subdue the impact of abuse? Most of the above are initial thoughts addressed in therapy, and fear is what separates people from separating the realistic versus unrealistic path to healing their pain. You must lean into your feelings as opposed to running from them—Easier said than done. Unfortunately, we find multiple reasons to circumvent facing our problem(s). "I'm too far gone." "It's hopeless." "It's really not that bad." "He did not mean what he said." "She is going to change." Deep inside, you know you are lying to yourself and enabling a cycle of pain and dysfunction. This is called, "Denial." The more time spent in denial, the more ingrained you become in your problem(s), hence the more you believe your delusions are acceptable ways to live. You must be transparent with yourself and face the realities which are preventing positive change. Are you afraid of what would happen if your desire to be free became true? Afraid of what your life would look like without the narcissist? Would you miss the relationship? Does your fear of change outweigh the decision to make better choices and leave the toxic person?" Sometimes, "Yes." Lean into these feelings, be honest with yourself, and work through the pain which prohibits healing. Most importantly, have hope. Without this, change is not possible.

Here are some steps to help you with your healing process:

<u>Acknowledge</u>: The first thing you must do is acknowledge you have been verbally, emotionally, and psychologically abused by the narcissist in your life. Patricia Evans, (2010, pg. 150) states in her book: *The Verbally Abusive Relationship: How to Recognize It and Respond*, "Recovery from verbal abuse is the opportunity to accept all your feelings and to recognize their validity." Accepting that your relationship has been built upon manipulation, deceit, and abuse is difficult and will take strength to admit. No one likes to feel as if their life has been a mask used by someone to create or maintain a persona. Nor does anyone like to think their life has been controlled by someone with a personality disorder. There is shame, guilt, and feelings of disappointment in themselves for not knowing exactly what was happening, not leaving sooner, or not rescuing their kids from the narcissist's abusive control. This is so difficult and one of the reasons a victim does not leave the narcissist sooner than later. Out of sight, out of mind. AKA – If they do not leave, the problem does not exist. Denying there was a problem and then not leaving after realizing there was a problem is difficult to accept. Therefore, acknowledging the truth years and even decades later is painful. However, the pain fades as the days pass and as the victim rewrites their life by living free from the abuser. Acknowledging the abuse in the beginning is the first step to healing. Attacking the abuse is a lifelong journey and way to freedom.

<u>Embrace Hope</u>: Hope is a feeling of expectation that something good will happen. It is a feeling which directs your state of mind for which is positively optimistic. Hope is "The belief your future can be brighter and better than your past and you have a role to play in making it better," (Gwinn, Casey and Hellman, Chan, 2021, pg. 9). I am honored to have had Dr. Chan Hellman as a professor of statistics at the University of Oklahoma and now a colleague. He is one of the leading Hope researchers in America and understands the overwhelming need to believe in a better future. Without hope, efforts to change your situation are futile. This can lead to self-destructive thinking such as, blaming yourself, settling for what could be better and healthier, and you may accept whatever happens to you as beyond your control. This is how the narcissist would like you to feel. It allows them to remain in control. However, the narcissist cannot take away your hope.

<u>Get professional help</u>: There is nothing more daunting than seeking professional help after being abused and wounded by a narcissist. It can be embarrassing, humiliating, and you may feel too broken to ask for help. You may feel as if no one will believe your story because of the twisted experiences you have endured. This is not true. Those in the mental health field have treated many who have struggled or are struggling with the reality of living with a narcissist. As you are searching for a therapist, you should inquire as to their specialty and specifically ask if they are experienced with victims of abuse, trauma, and personality disorders—specifically Narcissism. Additionally, there are trauma support groups overflowing with victims who have been emotionally,

physically, and mentally abused by a narcissist. This is a safe place where you can tell your story without judgment, shame, or fear of appearing insane.

Journal: Write about your personal feelings and experiences. There is no script, and no audience. Don't think about what you are going to write, how you are going to say it, or if you are even good enough of a writer to write. Journaling is a tool that is useful, as it helps to exercise the mind and detoxify your emotions. It will help you process your everyday stress, work through trauma caused by the narcissist, and navigate your therapy sessions if you are in mental health counseling. Writing can unmask feelings which have been repressed or denied. This is very important because the mind can and will call on its natural defense mechanisms to elevate emotional and mental self-preservation. When faced with a toxic situation or ongoing traumatic events, cognitive adaption occurs in which abusive behaviors are rationalized by assigning a different meaning which is justified or denied. This is also called, "Survival mode." If you convince yourself the abuse isn't "Abuse," you have not faced your reality, (and what feels like), the hopeless struggle to escape. Writing your feelings on paper brings an unabated truth of emotions to the surface – to bring denial and oppressed feelings to the surface.

1. ***Review your writings***. As painful as this will be, facing the abuse on paper will not only validate your choice to leave, but help you see the person you were without the psychological defenses getting in the way of long-term healthy choices and living free from your abuser.

2. ***Write a letter to your abuser***. First things first: Once you begin this letter, do NOT edit it. This letter should be raw. Do not hesitate to write your unfiltered thoughts in a way which mirrors your feelings. This may or may not be easy. It will depend upon the mindset you have when you begin the letter. Regardless, this is a safe place to tell the narcissist how you feel about what they have done to you and those around you. It is a place where you can be emotionally transparent without being told your "Feelings aren't valid," "You should not feel that way," or that "You are crazy." Write knowing you and only you will read it unless you choose otherwise. This is a healing process by which you are purging the emotional poison which has controlled your life. You are eliminating emotions which will hold you back from moving forward, while at the same time opening space to build a future grounded in positivity. **Do not give the letter to them!** For a narcissist, negative attention is better than no attention. Hence, avoid getting sucked into their attempts to create conflict. Below is a letter from a victim of a covert narcissist:

Dear Joe,

I want to begin this letter by telling you it is for me and not you. This letter is intended to expose you for who you are as an emotional abuser and Covert Narcissist. I am a voice for those who still have no idea as to who you are, and for those who could become victims of your mental illness. I will start from the beginning; with your "Story." You told me long ago your mother was a "Monster" and had mental health issues which caused you to lean in and be the caregiver to your brother and sister as a teenager. You explained she was abusive, yet heroic in that she, "Worked three jobs to keep you and your siblings in clothes without the help of your father. You moved from house to house because you mother always struggled with finances. With each move, the living conditions were worse. The size of the homes also decreased in size making it almost impossible to live." I felt sorry for you, while at the same time applauded your perseverance, motivation to succeed, and the self-confidence which was apparent in your identity as a result of your struggles as a child.

I heard this story for years as it was told to new people and told as a reminder to those who already knew it at Christmas parties, on holidays, and at casual dinners with friends. You would find a way to insert parts of your life story when the discussion allowed you to make an analogy to that of another person. You could not stand someone other than you, being the center of attention. Looking back, it reminds me of a three-year-old who wants their mother's attention as she is trying to talk with someone other than the child. I heard this story for years, and with each dialogue, it grew in length and gravity. The story was riveting and gained a lot of sympathy in the beginning of our relationship, but it took a decade to learn you were embellishing the story each time you told it. It was a good story though. You gained a lot of attention from others and the audience put you in a spotlight that was unique. We all have a "Story," but yours was used to gain idolatry and mesmerize a vulnerable audience. It took years of therapy for me to learn everything around you and anyone who was within your reach was used for your purpose. You were good at making others feel good about themselves but were disingenuous and a fraud. You used other people for your own purposes, gave them false hope, and used charisma to create magnetism. I wonder what it was like to live in your head of self-loathing while working so hard to gain acceptance. The energy you spent begging to be petted by everyone around you was pathetic. You lived in a world of your own self-hate and insecurity masked by lies, and deceit. I have since learned you even lied about graduating from college. Not all successes are made by attaining a college degree, but a good portion of successes are built upon hours of sitting through lectures, sleepless nights studying, writing, reading, and doing countless hours of research to validate your worth as a student, earn respect within the academic system, and leave knowing the efforts accomplished were worth it. However, for those of us who spent many years in school achieving collegiate goals and who use these credentials to gain respect, lying about having a college degree is pathetic– not to mention fraudulent, and criminal within the academic bylaws across most colleges – punishable. You are a disgrace in ways that have no measure. I have pity on you.

I suppose you are too wrapped up in yourself to see there are other onlookers who see your inauthenticity. These people are those who chose to not be pulled into your collection of people. Since I left you, I have learned there are many who don't trust or respect you. They have been in a relationship with you and left scared, (emotionally or financially). Your masks are many, but your favorite comes with a checkbook in hand and an illusional heart made of gold. You are a genius at making people feel good about themselves and safe when they are being recruited into your Harem – but you know this. You hunt and prey upon people who are in need and vulnerable. This also includes those at the top who can help you navigate your image, success, and perception of importance. As I look back, I see how your evil wrapped in a bow controls people and situations. This is your skill, and you will die knowing your reality was a creation by you based upon the delusion you were large and in charge when you were weak and desperate. This showed by the ways in which you used people and trapped them into believing you cared. As I look back, you had no one or anything which wasn't bought and paid for. Control, manipulation, and acting on your own stage are the only things which kept those who were close near. I have learned by watching your sickness evolve over the years. You were good at using distractions to throw me off so I would not leave you, and I didn't for a very long time. Dressing things and people up who were a part of your harem, was done well and must have been very taxing. Keeping all your lies, cheating, and tax evasion a secret required a certain level of mental gymnastics only a mental disordered person like yourself could navigate. But what I have always said, "Liars always get caught," which reminds me how you would become irate if anyone questioned your truth. No one had to use the word, "Liar." It did not even have to be insinuated.

 The thought of someone questioning your story or disagreeing with the recall of conversations would trigger indignance, and verbal intimidation delivered in the question, "Are you calling me a liar?!!!!!!" "Look at me!" "Are you calling me a liar?!!!!!!!" This became your platform when our son would catch you in a lie. He was fearless and could see through you. I find peace knowing you will never be successful at controlling him. As time has passed, he showed *me how strong his mind was when there was a risk of losing it when you were present. Is intuition learned or is it innate? In his case, it is both. This combined with his strength, independence, and observation of your actions has given him the ability to be around you without being fooled by your façade and caught in your web. Instead, I have witnessed him capitalize on your desperate need to control those who are close. He was never a long-term candidate for this, as he fought like Hell to avoid being victimized by your emotional manipulation. He somehow found a safe front row seat to your show without getting pulled into the production. I suspect there are others who also placate to your ego to achieve their own agenda. You will never accept that you are being played a fool because this dismantles your entire view of who you believe yourself to be. As I have physically distanced myself and emotionally detached from you, my eyes are fully open and I see you for the sad self you are and have always been. I hope and pray every day our children break free from your unseen emotional abuse. It is through forgiveness, strength, and hope I finally found* freedom." – Anonymous

Burn the letter to your abuser. Have a ceremony in which you watch your past life die. Think of this as purifying your life as you see your past disappear into the earth.

Find a Support Group. It is important to process your trauma in healthy ways. Holding in or trying to bypass the pain of trauma can lead to other mental health issues and/or adversely affect relationships. There are many online support groups designed to help people who have been victimized by narcissists. If you prefer to meet in-person, locate a mental health trauma specialist. They will be able to direct you to a group through their network of professional contacts. It is particularly comforting to talk with others who can fully understand what you have been through as a victim of narcissistic abuse. Their stories will be like yours and some may appear to be much worse. There is no way to measure or place a value on trauma, because trauma is trauma. However, emotional manipulation takes on varying constructs of pain, wears different masks, and no two stories are exactly alike. Learning it is okay to tell your story with people who can identify with your trauma is powerful. You will finally feel validated and grounded. Equally important is feeling confident telling your story without feeling others think you are crazy or exaggerating. Anyone who has told their story or sought out help after getting into an argument with a narcissist knows it is inherently impossible for others to understand the insanity unless they too have been hurt by a narcissist.

Create a Routine and Goals: This will help you feel as if you are starting over and putting the past behind you. Make a list of the things you would like to do if you had the resources to make it happen. I say this only because we often use cynicism to deter us from taking risks or self-sabotage our hopes and dreams by looking downward as opposed to up and into the future. If you want to be or do something which you feel you cannot because you don't have a pathway to get there, reconsider. We can find ways to achieve our goals if we have faith in ourselves to navigate the goal.

Practice Mindfulness. I suggest this because there are many tools available that will help you process trauma in a way that feels safe and controlled. "Mindfulness" has been assigned many definitions, but the common theme is embracing an awareness of the present and freely accepting one's feelings and thoughts as they enter the mind.

There are several ways in which mindfulness can help relax your body while addressing the stress and anxiety caused by your trauma. It has been known to slow down the thoughts which are triggering heightened states of emotional distress. Meditation is used to help those who struggle with anxiety, obsessive compulsive disorder, and panic attacks caused by trauma. Research the different forms of meditation before you begin, as there is an array of methods; finding the right one for you is important. Once you have determined this, be patient. It may feel awkward at first, but with practice and education about healing through self-awareness, you will feel yourself slowly take back your life.

Yoga is a form of mindfulness. It is a place where you can calmly acknowledge your thoughts in a safe setting. This is a comforting place which allows uncovered thoughts to manifest in which you have repressed by disassociating from the trauma. Stearns and Stearns, (2012, pg., 125) state, "Disassociation is the reaction that occurs when threatening circumstances overwhelm your ability to cope." This is our body's natural defense mechanisms seeking to protect our emotions from the pain caused by trauma. Jackson MacKenzie, (cofounder of schopathfree.com) states, "This is what your body does to protect you from emotional trauma and shame. It doesn't yet have the tools to heal those things, so it numbs them, pushes them away on your body, and routes you around them," (2019, pg. 141). For the purposes of this book, the body's self-perseverance response is reacting to shield you from the emotional trauma caused by narcissistic abuse. Learning to be in the present both physically and emotionally, as opposed to repressing the past while living in it at the same time should be a goal. Yoga can be beneficial to your overall wellness and help you heal from emotional abuse. There are many distinct types of yoga. If you have never practiced yoga,

I suggest a form of yoga that is geared towards relaxation. Yoga Nidra is good form of yoga to begin with, geared towards beginners. It seeks to ease you into a state of deep relaxed consciousness that flows between sleep and wakefulness. Yoga Nidra uses guided meditation to induce a state of near-sleep. It helps to reduce stress, anxiety and help you sleep if you struggle with anxious thoughts at night. There are many forms of yoga specific to emotional trauma. Before beginning a method of yoga, do your research to determine what speaks to you. I also suggest looking into mind and body trauma classes that integrate yoga into their healing programs.

Exercise and nutrition are forms of mindfulness. Physical movement is one of the most powerful ways to feel free and in control of your mind. It helps regulate mood, stabilize anxiety, and provides an overall sense of healthy cognition. Research has shown exercise is equally as important to the brain as it is to the body. What impacts the mind impacts the body and vice-versa. Therefore, exercise should be a property in mental health treatment following traumatic events. Making it a part of the healing process is instrumental, as exercise naturally reduces depression, helps with insomnia, regulates mood, rebuilds self-confidence, claims ownership of the body, and helps provide structure which can help facilitate the creation of a new and better self.

Food is one of those things many people bypass or don't consider when trying to navigate mental health. It is probably not the first thing which comes to mind when trying to identify methods to assist you on our journey to finding better mental health. Nutrition has always been and will always be a staple in the trajectory of our emotional, mental, and physical wellbeing. Food is comprised of chemicals with healing properties and chemicals with addictive properties. Many survivors of abuse use food to cope with trauma. They will eat or binge on foods that contain high levels of sugar and little nutritional value. Foods such as chocolate, cake, ice cream, and cookies are addictive due to high levels of sugar and your brain's response to sugar. Sugar creates emotional highs which trigger short-term feelings of satisfaction that send the brain and body into a state of wanting more. Naturally, repetitive behaviors can be addictive or become addictive. The result of this can lead to addiction and eating disorders. Unfortunately, this coincides with the narcissist's goal to emotionally abuse you by sabotaging your self-image, leading to self-hate and self-loathing. I am not suggesting you must not ever eat sugar. In fact, it is a proven fact dark chocolate in moderation helps to boost mood. It will also help regulate bodily functions affected by stress and trauma. As just mentioned, foods also have healing properties which have the power to help you cope with trauma. For example, Salmon contains fatty acids which are associated with lower levels of sadness and depression. Certain fruits such as bananas contain probiotics which help to feed bacteria in the gut. Probiotics help to promote gut health and mood because of the live microorganisms that help develop healthy bacteria in the gut. I am simply asking you to be aware of how much sugar is in the foods that you are compelled to eat. Furthermore, be emotionally present. This means, try to recognize your feelings before you go to the refrigerator or pantry. Lastly, it will be helpful if you take the time to meal plan. Not only does this help you guide your journey in a systematic way, but it forces you to focus on the task at hand leaving you less time to ruminate about the trauma. Every little bit of time it takes to rebuild your life is taking away from the brokenness caused by the narcissist.

Meditation: embracing private time is a powerful way to take back control of your life. "The greatest weapon against stress is our ability to choose one thought over another." This is a quote from the famous philosopher and psychologist William James who is responsible for psychology as a formal discipline.

Medications: What about medication? Some people prefer to take medications because they believe it will be the cure for their pain. In his book, *The Body Keeps the Score*, (2015, pg. 226)." Dr. Van Der Kolk, M.D. states, "Drugs cannot "cure" trauma; they can only dampen the expressions of a disturbed physiology. And they do not teach the lasting lessons of self-regulation." He goes on to say, "They can help control feelings and behavior but always at a price – because they work by blocking the chemical systems that regulate engagement, motivation, pain, and pleasure." There is a time and place for medications, but not everyone needs to rely on drugs to take their life back from trauma. I am not a psychiatrist, and I am not claiming that medication cannot help and even be a staple in a person's process of healing from abuse. I am suggesting you talk to a qualified doctor about the long-term effects of medication, chances of chemical and psychological dependence, and what your future goals are as it relates to your overall health.

Take back your identity: It is likely you cannot see this happening. You may feel hopeless, insecure, and question your ability to make yourself whole again and stronger after the trauma. As I write this, I am giving you the confidence and strength to use on your journey to heal. You will recover successfully, and you will rebuild yourself by actively using coping strategies which address both your brain and body. I have discussed many of these tools above and hope you use parts of each strategy which speak to you in a positive way. Creating a stronger self is best developed by taking the old parts of yourself and placing them in a healthy place. As I mentioned earlier, you will never forget the narcissist who took parts of you away and used you to shape their own identity. I am a firm believer putting the memories and the narcissist in place is known but not felt – every day is important. There is a difference between forgetting and forgiving. Furthermore, trying to forget circumvents positive energy which can be utilized for healing and is driven by resentment, anger, and hate. These emotions feed the trauma and can be enjoyable for the narcissist to watch, if they are lingering around because you share kids. The best revenge is ignoring the narcissist and being happy without them. However, do not do this for the sole purpose of hurting the narcissist, because everything you do moving forward is owned by you and used to rebuild your life. If you embrace this, emancipation from the narcissist naturally evolves and the rejection felt by the narcissist is excruciating and inevitably real. If you started reading this book having a fraction of hope, you are off to a good start. However, you probably are still in search for ways to guide lingering uncertainty, feelings of insecurity, fear, and distrust.

LET THEM HAVE THEIR GLORY

Once you have fully disengaged, detached, and found peace from the narcissist, let them have their glory. This means, when they prance and flex to gain attention from others, roll your eyes. Realize this is who they are, and sadly, who they will always be. Their egos and self-worth are highly dependent upon other's affirmation and approval. This will not change because there is no internal compass guiding healthy self-awareness. They are also lacking in emotional security, or self-confidence. Like most of us, we know when we have pushed too far or made a fool out of ourselves. This comes with a general feeling of embarrassment and oftentimes shame. This is not true for the narcissist. They do not live in the same reality. The narcissist is under the illusion others are constantly looking at them in admiration and envy. Remember their detachment is due to their constant obsession with themselves and the ways in which they believe they are perceived. Once you have freed yourself from this, you can sit back and watch the show. A large part of this is watching the theatrics which persist within their Harem. The collection of people who the narcissist has chosen to affirm his manufactured greatness and his accomplishments, (AKA the Narcissist's Supply) will change as people come and go, depending upon their allegiance to the narcissist. Yes, people do leave the narcissist on occasion because they are tipped off or rubbed the wrong way by something the narcissist has said or done. Jamieson, (2021, pg. 117) states, "The paradox is, that they may be superb at winning us over in the short term, but in the longer term, the wheels will always come off." Where there is deception, there is also a truth. Watch their self-destruction from afar and be happy you are no longer a part of narcissist's self-identity and demise. You will be able to clearly see the toxicity within the manipulative webs which are woven to control others. Although it may be difficult to watch because someone you love or care about does not understand their vulnerability to their narcissist abuser, know the person(s) you love will outgrow the narcissist and leave, just as you did. This will help you to better understand your own struggles, the pain for which you have overcome, and regain your identity. Living with the confidence and strength you deserve will help you see and feel your potential to live.

    Learning to date and love again are two things which feel daunting and even terrifying. You should not enter this process until you have had time to heal and had closure with the past trauma from a narcissist. This is important because you need to be clear minded, and fully understand why and how you became involved with the narcissist. You may benefit from:

Psychoanalysis which encompasses looking into childhood experiences and relationships which were emotionally abusive but, were made to be thought of as loving. You may also learn your relationship with a narcissist began as a child because you were forced into the role of being a parent to a narcissistic parent.

Cognitive Behavioral Therapy looks to help a client identify thoughts, behaviors, and attitudes which reflect negatively in one's life. This form of therapy can be helpful for victims who inflict self-harm upon their bodies. Victims (mostly young women) of abuse often self-harm. Cutting body parts, pulling out hair, and obsessive nail biting are a few behaviors which qualify.

Eye Movement Desensitization and Processing, (EMDR) is a form of trauma-based therapy which helps people focus on their trauma by being visually stimulated. EMDR is somewhat new and like psychoanalytic therapy it helps to identify trapped memories in the body's nervous system. Those who suffer from PSTD are often led to this form of therapy as are others who struggle with other forms of trauma.

Brain Spotting Therapy helps to identify trauma, emotional pain and psychologically induced physical pain.

Group Therapy is helpful because it is reassuring to know you are not alone. Often victims of narcissists feel alienated and hesitate to speak up because the emotional abuse is so deep and the horrific stories about it sound exaggerated or made up. Learning of this will take time and discipline in and out of the therapy room.

You will most certainly work within therapy models which address trauma. Whatever form of therapy you use, make for certain it is evidence-based. A positive thing to recognize is recovery is within reach and establishing independence and feeling secure in your future life choices will occur.

FINDING LOVE AFTER HEALING

It isn't until you meet someone who is emotionally healthy you fully understand the degree to which you were abused by a narcissist. Your friends and family will be relieved you finally left. There are things you need to know to protect yourself from being victimized by another person with the same toxic needs.

1) **Enter a relationship slowly** – You should be capable of being alone and know you have healed from the trauma. To get to this place, collaborate with a professional mental health therapist who can objectively navigate this journey. You cannot understand what love is if you are still living in the mental space of being brainwashed.
2) **Be observant** – Some of the things which appeared to be qualities or assets within narcissist personality are most likely red flags. Closely assess the context for which they act on their decisions. For example. What is the context behind their priorities or goals? Are they motivated by social acceptance, control, or greed? Any of these answers should be a warning signal to turn the other way.
3) **Proceed with caution** – When you meet another person who you connect with, it may feel as if you are living in a dream.

You might not know how to act. This can be confusing and scary. Sorting through this may take some time, because you are coming out of a toxic relationship with someone who was not trustworthy or emotionally available. At some point though, trust your intuition. You do not always need to rely on self-help books or advise from others to become whole again. Trusting yourself is part of owning your power and the freedom to make healthy decisions in all areas of your life. Allowing others in your space and life is a privilege and there is nothing like having the confidence to say, "No" if you do not feel safe or "Yes" if they will add pleasure and happiness to your life. As it pertains to allowing people in your life, trust your feelings as you intuit a positive or negative energy sent in your direction.

4) **Have optimism** – It is important to know there are good people out in the world who are safe and emotionally healthy. You will find love and feel good about your decisions to choose those who you feel safe with. Love will come to you. You deserve to be happy and will as you find yourself and grow within. Strength, confidence, and perseverance are the things which provide survival in a world which is not always safe from those who live to capitalize on other's weaknesses. They are out there, and they prey upon those who are vulnerable. You are no longer that person, and of no interest to the narcissistic desires of people who are mentally ill. Loving yourself and embracing the path of self-survival will drive relationship success. You will feel the emotional shift within yourself, and you will be available to share your life and love with someone who is deserving of you. It will happen.

*Finding love within yourself overflows into
loving someone else.
Dr. Courtney Linsenmeyer-O'Brien, Ph.D.*

TRUST YOUR INSTINCTS

A client of mine once said, "Anything that is hard to get is worth having, and anything that is easy to get isn't worth having." I thought this was profound and perfect for this book, as overcoming the trauma caused by a narcissist is not an easy journey. It is one of the most difficult forms of abuse to heal from and this is only if you can escape their captivity. The good news is leaving is possible – if you can see the person in your life is not who they said they were in the beginning. Sadly, due to the manipulation and emotional abuse which distorted your feelings of security, it will take time for you to notice the person you are involved with is a narcissist. In her documentary, "Divorcing a Narcissist: One Mom's Battle," Tina Swithin states, "The moral of the story is, your intuition is never wrong," (2018, pg. 25). There is one thing we cannot deny, our innate ability to intuit feelings of safety and risk. Some of us are better than others at identifying emotional danger, and narcissists are acutely aware of emotional vulnerability. Therefore, the narcissist targets those who don't see them coming. Regardless, when something feels off, it is. This is why you should consider the opinions of those who are close to you and care about your wellbeing. Your family and friends won't lie after seeing the abuse and trauma you have endured. Remember growth requires fully understanding yourself, having closure with your past, and having the confidence to move forward. People are attracted to self-confidence and feed off other's self-esteem. You must be able to distinguish between those who are fake and those who are truly stable.

Listen to your instincts. Abuse never feels, "Right."
Dr. O'Brien, Ph.D.

LEARN FAITH

When you have made the decision to abandon the narcissist for good, you must have faith and be optimistic about your ability to successfully leave and stay away from the narcissist. It is easier if you define what faith means to you. Faith gives us purpose, protects us, and provides meaning to our lives. It will give you confidence, strength, and a trust in yourself which propels hope. Understand hope and faith are complimentary. One gives us the optimism that something good will happen and the other gives us a deeper confidence the hope we have is more likely to surface if we place more confidence in a belief system. Simply put, faith is something grounded in the reality of hope, and hope is a feeling of desire and expectation for a particular thing to occur. One cannot operate without the other.

The word, "Hope" I take for faith; And indeed, hope is nothing else but the constancy of faith.
John Calvin

CONCLUSION

RIDING THE WAVE OF BEING FREE

I sincerely hope this book has filled an objective and helped you facilitate a change or achieve an agenda you have been seeking. It was meant to help you navigate your circumstances in ways which provide hope for a better life after experiencing trauma from inside of a relationship with a narcissist. It is never easy to journey yourself out of a toxic relationship. The path is difficult to say the least. It is emotionally draining, psychologically complex, and feels hopeless at times. If you have already attempted to escape from the torment, it is likely you already know this. A client once told me, "Trying to leave my husband and break through the emotional damage he inflicted feels as if I am trying to find my way out of a dark hole without a ladder." If you have escaped the grips of a narcissist and are working towards a better and more loving life, do not look back or ask yourself if you did the right thing. Abuse is never the "Right thing." Likewise, leaving them is always the right thing. It will take time away from the narcissist to understand you do not need them in the ways they once made you feel dependent. They are not good at creating relationships which do not feed on co-dependency. Not healing or seeking closure allows an invisible connection to remain.

You do not want this. If their emotional presence is still lingering in your life, you are still giving your past space the room to interfere with your future. Unlearning dependency is difficult and can feel empty. Fall into yourself. This means to learn it is okay to be yourself and bury the life you once lived with the narcissist. Use your newfound freedom to build, grow, and establish the strength within yourself which you have always had.

RETRIBUTION

If you want retribution, write a book.

THE END

NOTES/REFERENCES

1. Beharym, Wendy, LCSW, (2013, pg. 28); Disarming the Narcissist: surviving & Thriving with The Self-Absorbed.
2. Evans, Patricia, (2010, pg. 150); The Verbally Abusive Relationship: How to Recognize It and How to Respond.
3. Gwinn, Casey & Hellman, Chan, Ph.D. (2021, pg. 9); Hope Rising: How the Science of Hope can Change Your Life.
4. Hollman, Laurie, PhD. (2020, pg. 11); Are You Living with a Narcissist? How Narcissistic Men Impact Your Happiness, How to Identify Them, and How to Avoid Raising One.
5. Jamieson, A.B. (2021, pg. 25, 29, 117); Prepare to Be Tortured: The Price You Will Pay for Dating a Narcissist.
6. Korten, David, (2015, pg. 1); How Narcissists Use Money to Abuse).
7. Lowen, MD, Alexander, (1997, pg. 84, 123); Narcissism: Denial of The True Self.
8. Maccoby, Michael, Harvard Business Review, (2004, pg.10); Narcissistic Leaders: The Incredible Pros, the Inevitable Cons.
9. MacKenzie, Jackson (2019, pg. 141); Whole Again: Healing Your Heart and Rediscovering Your True Self After Toxic Relationships and Emotional Abuse.

10. Mirza, Debbie, (2017, pg. 24); The Covert Passive Aggressive Narcissist: Recognizing the Traits and Finding Healing After Hidden Emotional and Psychological Abuse
11. Shahida, Theresa, (2019); Narcissism Books: 4 Manuscripts – Dealing with a Narcissist, Narcissistic Relationship, Narcissistic Abuse, and Narcissist Mothers.
12. Stearns M. N. & Stearns, R. N. (2013, pg. 125); Yoga for Emotional Trauma: Meditations and Practices for Healing Pain and Suffering.
13. Stinson, et al., (2008, pg. 1); DSM-5 – Narcissistic Personality Disorder: Symptom Expression Using IRT Response Theory (IRT).
14. Swithin, Tina, (2018, pg. 19, 23); Divorcing a Narcissist: One Mom's Battle.
15. Van Der Kolk, Bessel, (2014, pg. 226); The Body Keeps Score: Brain, Mind, and Body in the Healing of Trauma.

RECOMMENDED READINGS

1. The Art of Loving; (1956) by Erich Fromm.
2. The Sociopath Next Door; (2005) by Martha Stout.
3. The Covert Passive Aggressive Narcissist: Recognizing the Traits and Finding Healing After Hidden and Emotional and Psychological Abuse; (2017) by Debbie Miraz.
4. Worthy of Love: Reclaiming the Love of Who You Are; (2021) by Debbie Miraz.
5. Hidden Abuse: A Journey Through the Stages of Recovery from Psychological Abuse; (2016) by Shannon Thomas.
6. When Loving Him is Hurting You: Hope and Help for Women Who Are Dealing with Narcissism and Emotional Abuse; (2017) by Dr. David Hawkins, PhD.
7. Snakes In Suites: When Psychopaths Go to Work; (2006) by Dr. Paul Babiak, Ph.D. and Robert D. Hare, Ph.D.
8. Love Is Letting Go of Fear; (2011) by Gerald, G. Jampolsky, MD.
9. Mayo Clinic Family Health Book: Fifth Edition; (2022). Https://order.store.Mayoclinic.com